INSTANT Piano Songs

Audio Access
Included

POP HITS
Simple Sheet Music + Audio Play-Along

T0079418

PLAYBACK+
Speed • Pitch • Balance • Loop

To access audio visit:
www.halleonard.com/mylibrary

Enter Code
4943-0458-2121-1234

ISBN 978-1-5400-3596-7

HAL•LEONARD®

Visit Hal Leonard Online at
www.halleonard.com

Contact Us:
Hal Leonard
7777 West Bluemound Road
Milwaukee, WI 53213
Email: info@halleonard.com

In Europe contact:
Hal Leonard Europe Limited
42 Wigmore Street
Marylebone, London, W1U 2RN
Email: info@halleonardeurope.com

In Australia contact:
Hal Leonard Australia Pty. Ltd.
4 Lentara Court
Cheltenham, Victoria, 3192 Australia
Email: info@halleonard.com.au

CONTENTS

4   INTRODUCTION

6   **All of Me**
John Legend

12 **Can't Feel My Face**
The Weeknd

9   **Chasing Cars**
Snow Patrol

15 **Despacito**
Luis Fonsi & Daddy Yankee
feat. Justin Bieber

18 **Feel It Still**
Portugal. The Man

20 **Happy**
Pharrell Williams

26 **Havana**
Camila Cabello
feat. Young Thug

28 **Hello**
Adele

23 **Hey, Soul Sister**
Train

30 **Ho Hey**
The Lumineers

32 **I Knew You Were Trouble**
Taylor Swift

35 **I'm Yours**
Jason Mraz

38 **Just Give Me a Reason**
P!nk featuring Nate Ruess

41 **Let Her Go**
Passenger

47 **Lost Boy**
Ruth B

44 **Love Yourself**
Justin Bieber

50 **Million Reasons**
Lady Gaga

54 **One Call Away**
Charlie Puth

57 **100 Years**
Five for Fighting

60 **Perfect**
Ed Sheeran

73 **Riptide**
Vance Joy

64 **Say You Won't Let Go**
James Arthur

68 **See You Again**
Wiz Khalifa feat. Charlie Puth

70 **7 Years**
Lukas Graham

76 **Shake It Off**
Taylor Swift

82 **Stay with Me**
Sam Smith

84 **Thinking Out Loud**
Ed Sheeran

79 **Viva La Vida**
Coldplay

87 **What Makes You Beautiful**
One Direction

90 **You Are the Reason**
Calum Scott

Welcome to the *INSTANT Piano Songs* series!

This unique, flexible collection allows you to play with either one hand or two. Three playing options are available—all of which sound great with the online backing tracks:

1. **Play only the melody with your right hand.**

2. **Add basic chords in your left hand, which are notated for you.**

3. **Use suggested rhythm patterns for the left-hand chords.**

Letter names appear inside the notes in both hands to assist you, and there are no key signatures to worry about. If a **sharp** ♯ or **flat** ♭ is needed, it is shown beside the note each time, even within the same measure.

If two notes are connected by a **tie** ‿, hold the first note for the combined number of beats. (The second note does not show a letter name since it is not re-struck.)

Sometimes the melody needs to be played an octave higher to avoid overlapping with the left-hand chords. (If your starting note is C, the next C to the right is one octave higher.) If you are using only your right hand, however, you can disregard this instruction in the music.

🔊 The backing tracks are designed to enhance the piano arrangements, regardless of how you choose to play them. Each track includes two measures of count-off clicks at the beginning. If the recording is too fast or too slow, use the online **PLAYBACK+** player to adjust it to a more comfortable tempo (speed).

Optional left-hand rhythm patterns are provided for when you are ready to move beyond the basic chords. The patterns are based on the three notes of the basic chords and appear as small, gray notes in the first line of each song. Feel free to use the suggested pattern throughout the song, or create your own. Sample rhythm patterns are shown below. (Of course, you can always play just the basic chords if you wish!)

Have fun! Whether you play with one hand or two, you'll sound great!

Sample Rhythm Patterns

4/4 Meter

3/4 Meter

6/8 Meter

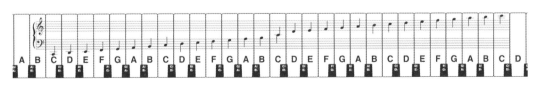

Also Available

Hal Leonard Student Keyboard Guide HL00296039

Key Stickers HL00100016

All of Me

Words and Music by John Stephens
and Toby Gad

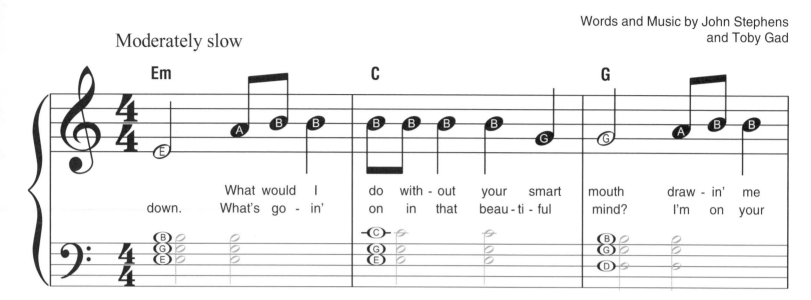

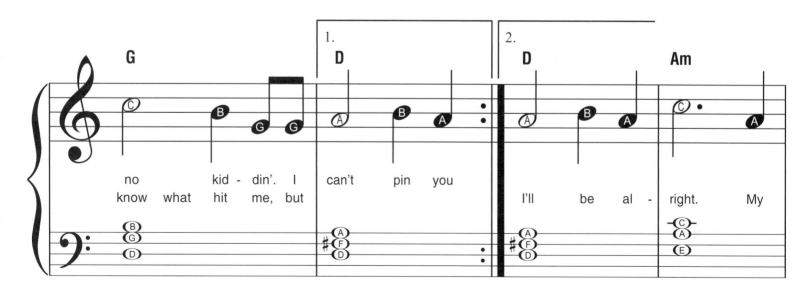

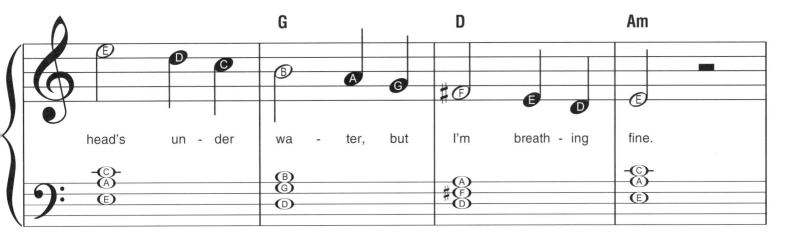

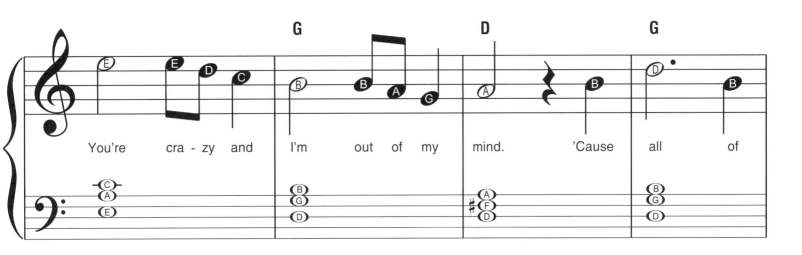

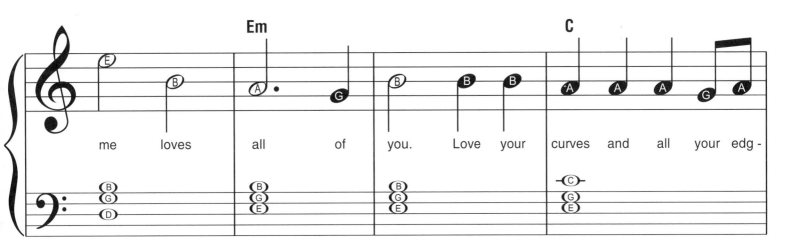

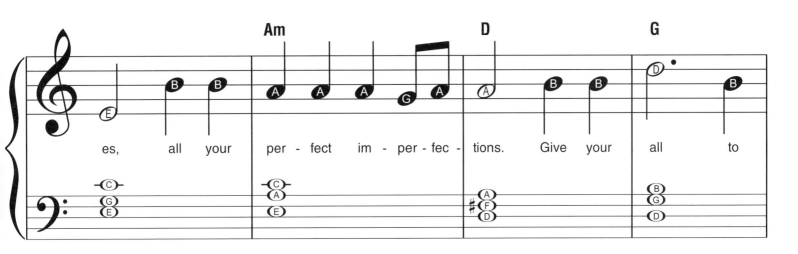

8

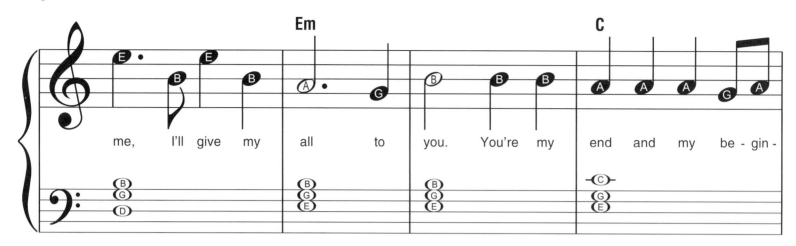

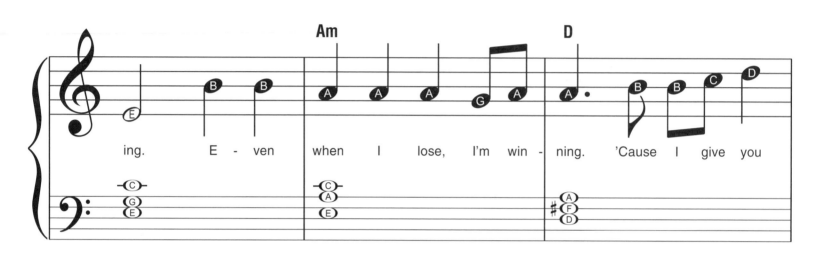

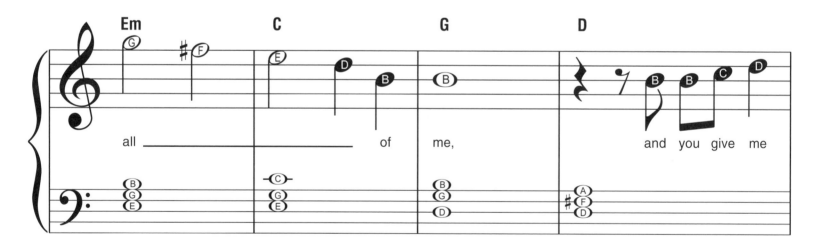

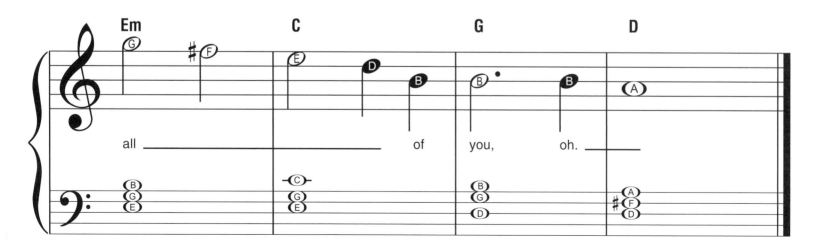

Chasing Cars

Words and Music by Gary Lightbody,
Tom Simpson, Paul Wilson,
Jonathan Quinn and Nathan Connolly

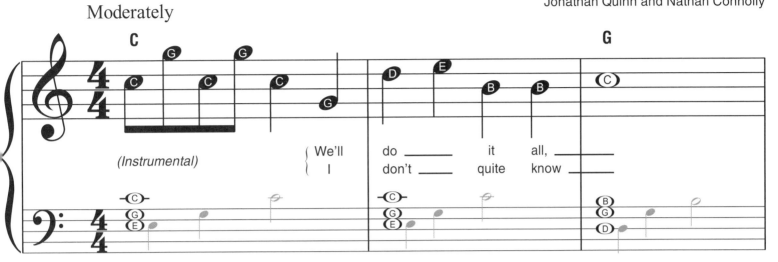

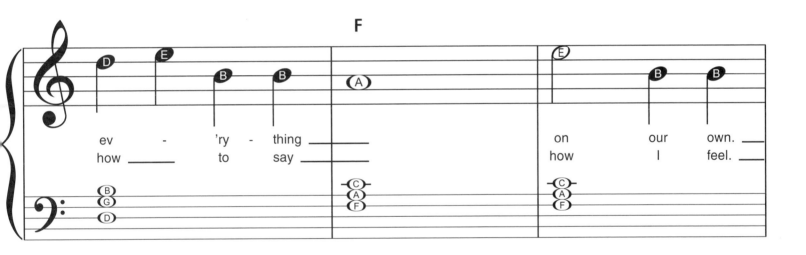

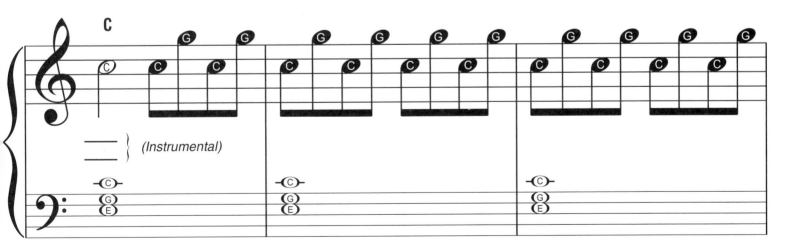

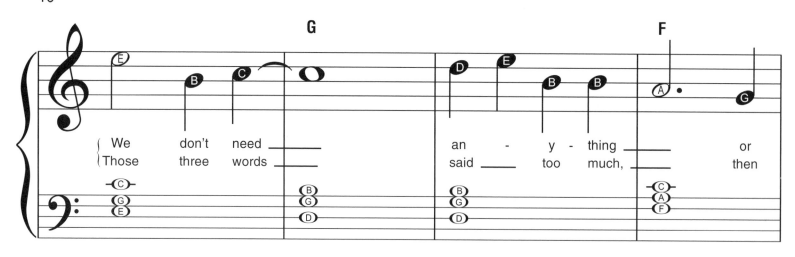

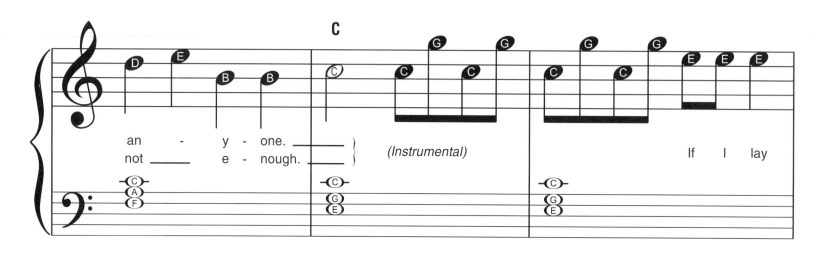

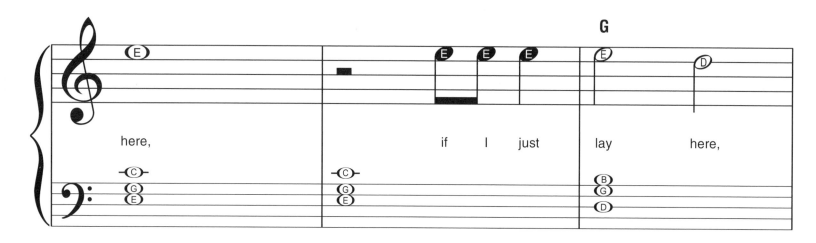

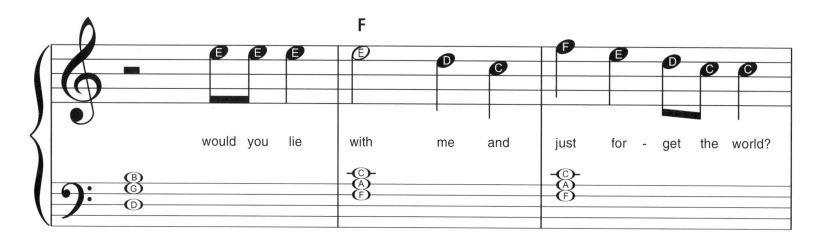

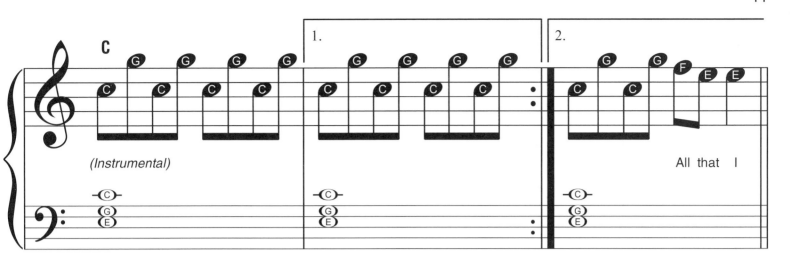

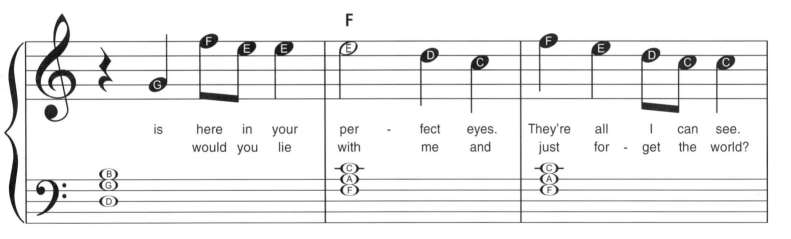

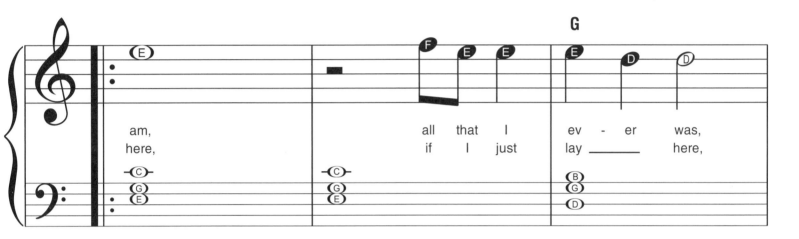

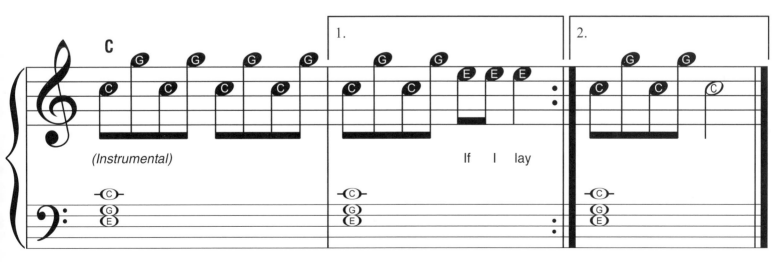

Can't Feel My Face

Words and Music by Abel Tesfaye,
Max Martin, Savan Kotecha,
Anders Svensson and Ali Payami

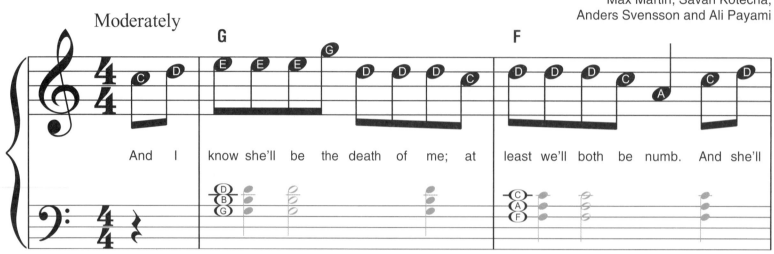

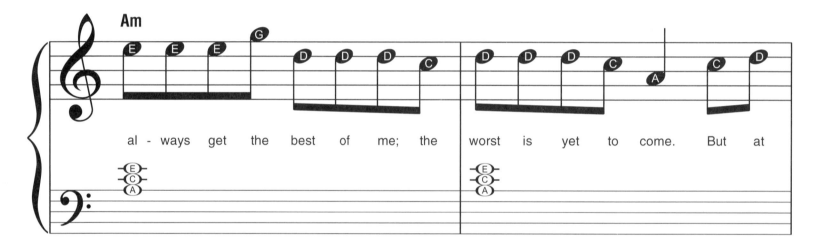

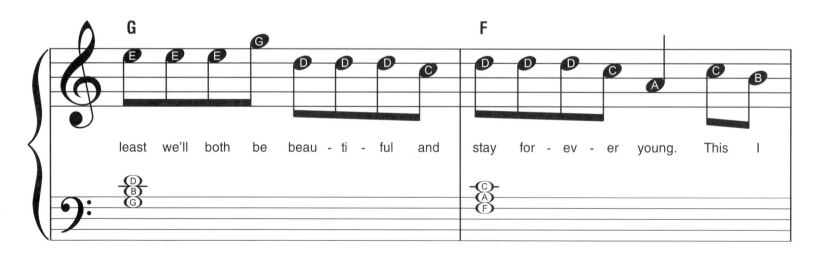

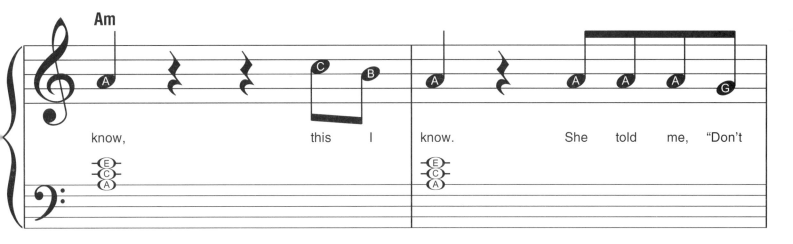

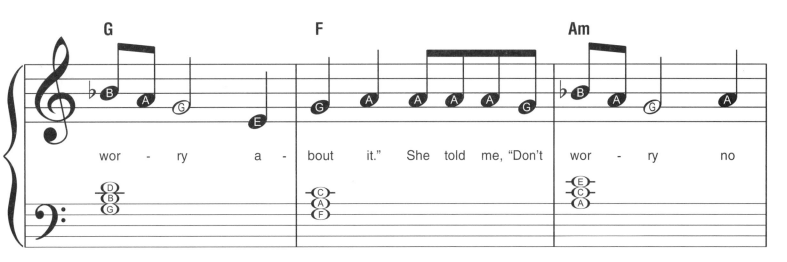

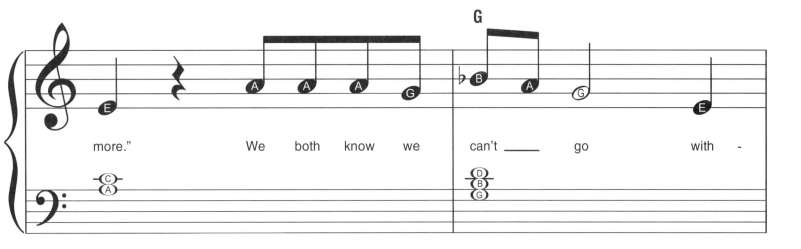

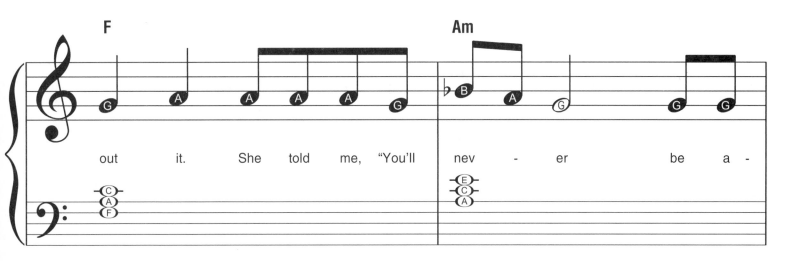

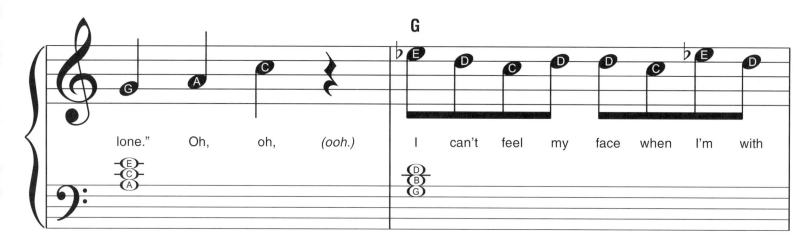

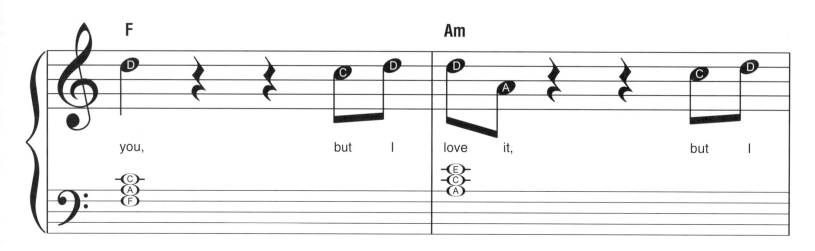

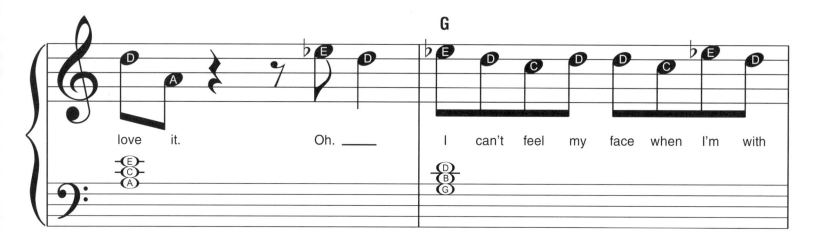

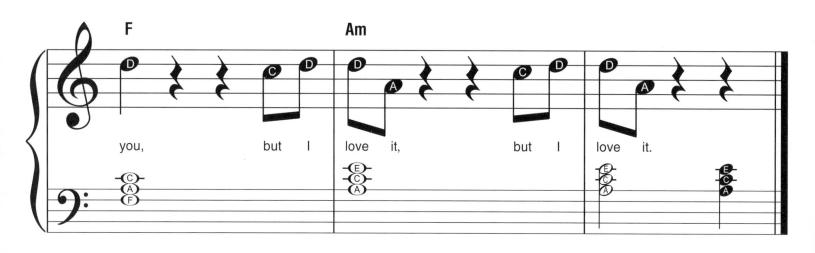

Despacito

Words and Music by Luis Fonsi,
Erika Ender, Justin Bieber,
Jason Boyd, Marty James Garton
and Ramón Ayala

Moderate Latin beat
(no chord)

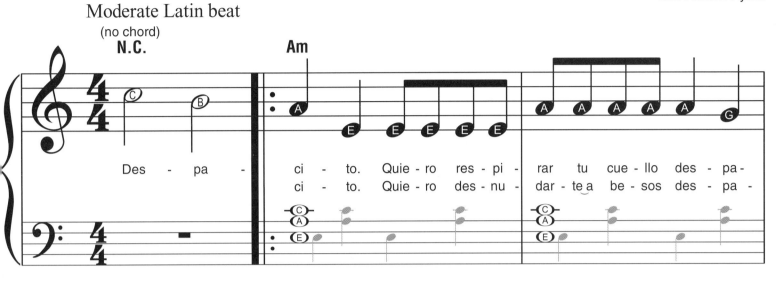

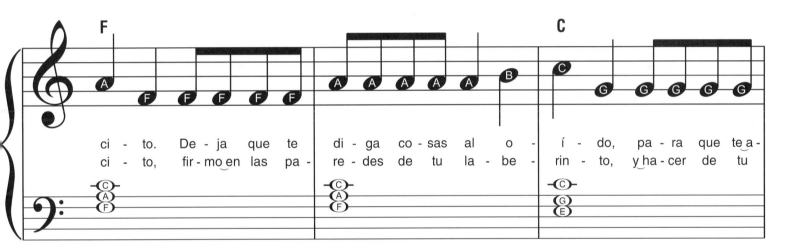

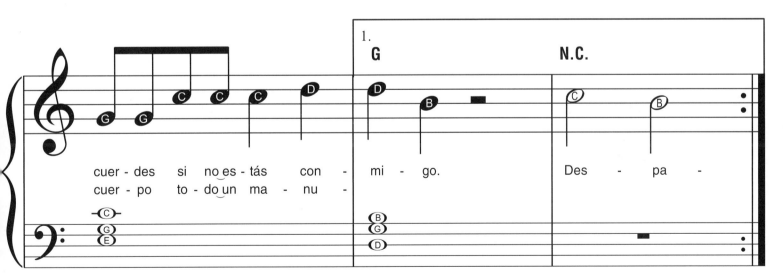

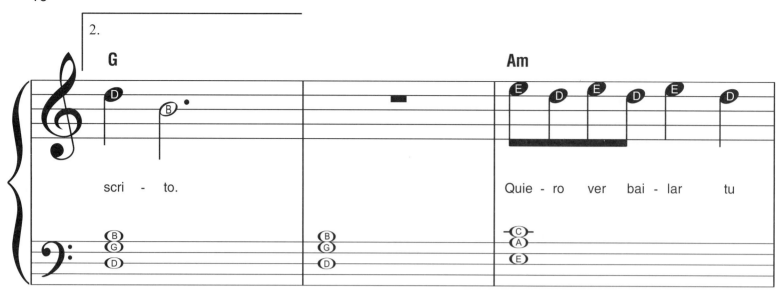

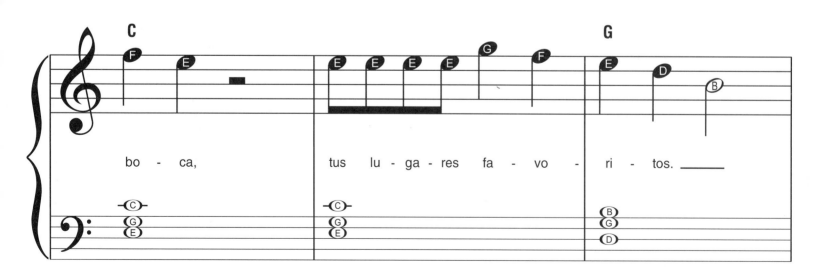

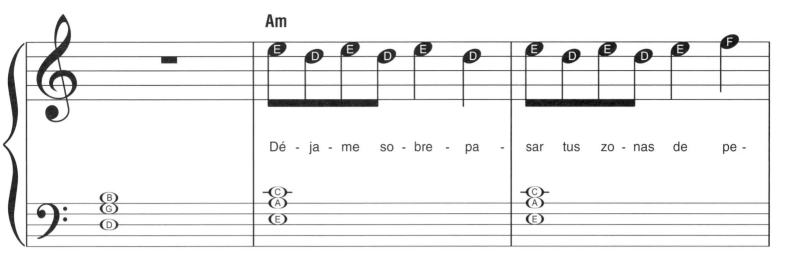

Dé - ja - me so - bre - pa - sar tus zo - nas de pe -

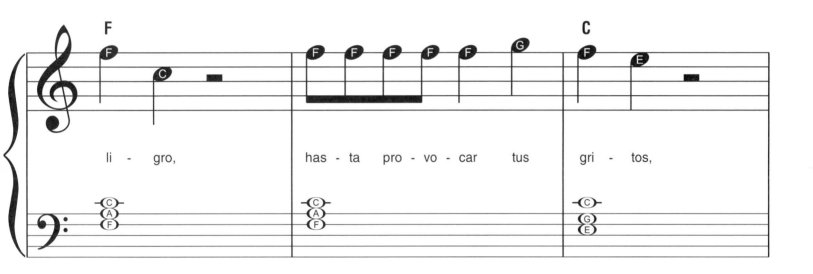

li - gro, has - ta pro - vo - car tus gri - tos,

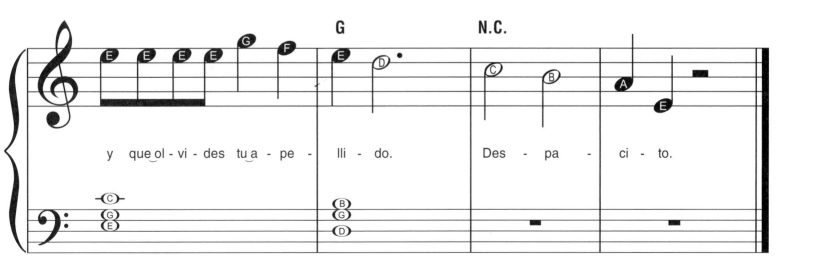

y que ol - vi - des tu a - pe - lli - do. Des - pa - ci - to.

Feel It Still

Words and Music by John Gourley,
Zach Carothers, Jason Sechrist,
Eric Howk, Kyle O'Quin,
Brian Holland, Freddie Gorman,
Georgia Dobbins, Robert Bateman,
William Garrett, John Hill and Asa Taccone

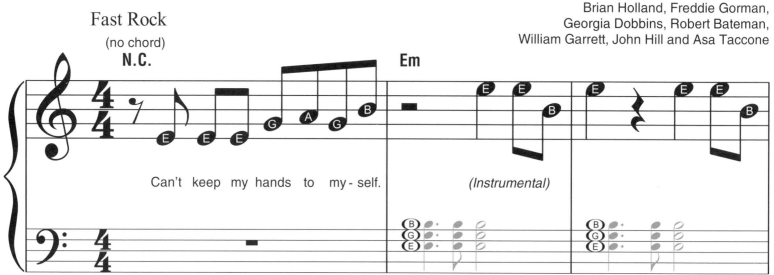

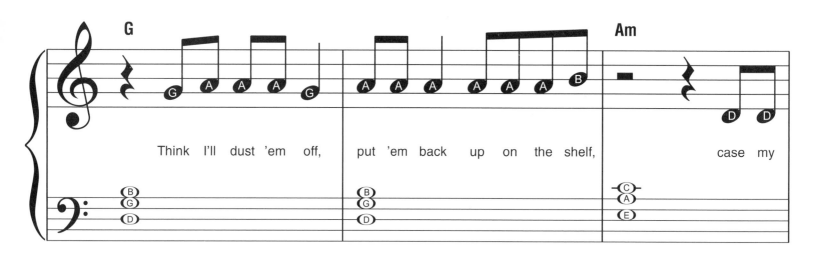

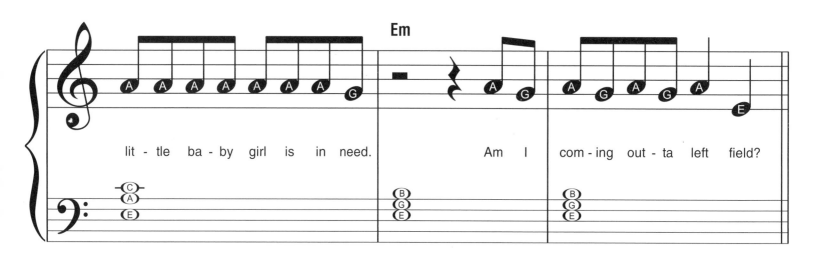

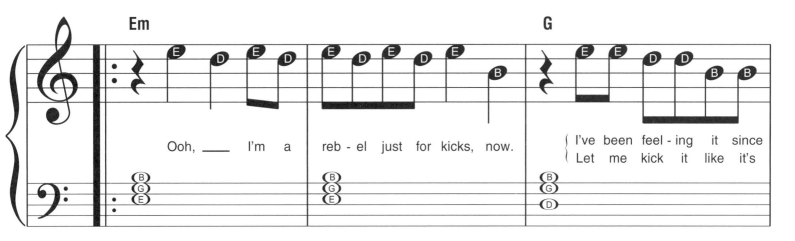

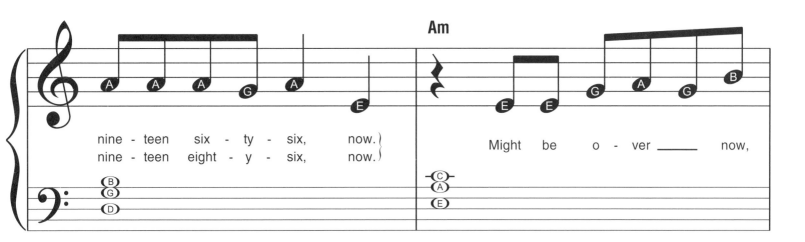

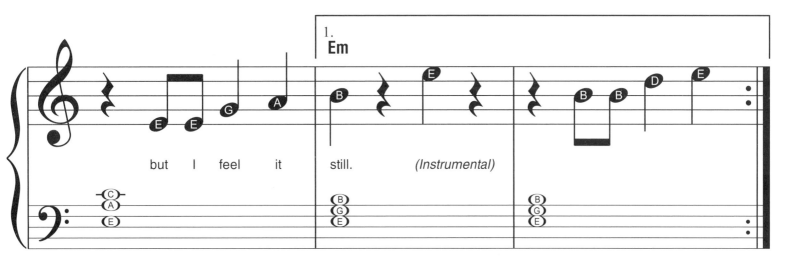

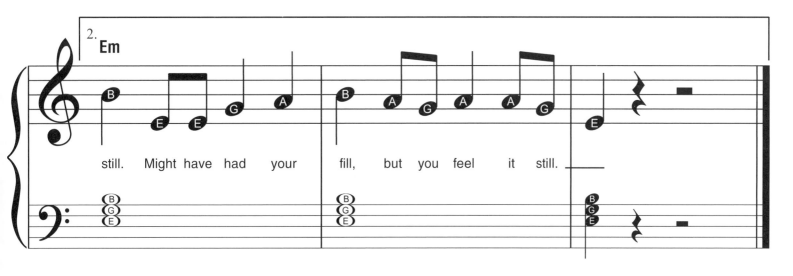

Happy
from DESPICABLE ME 2

Words and Music by
Pharrell Williams

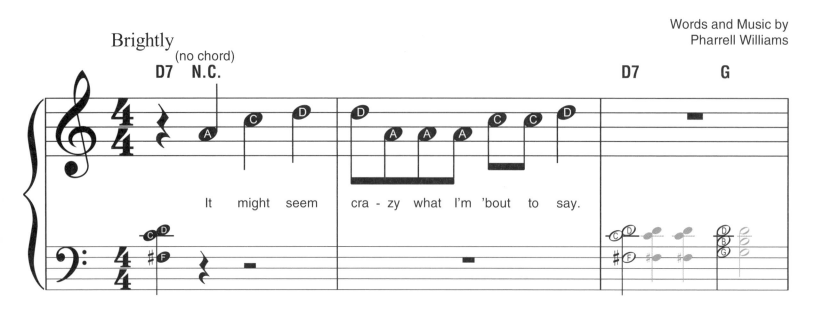

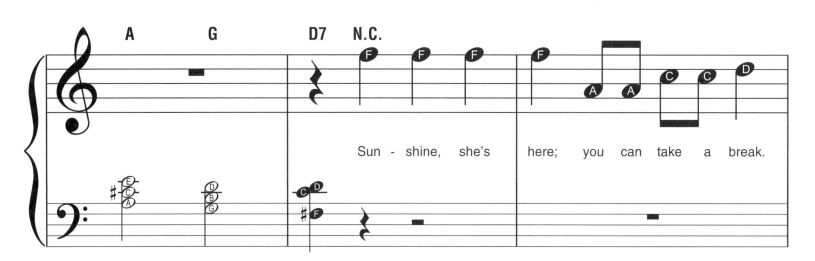

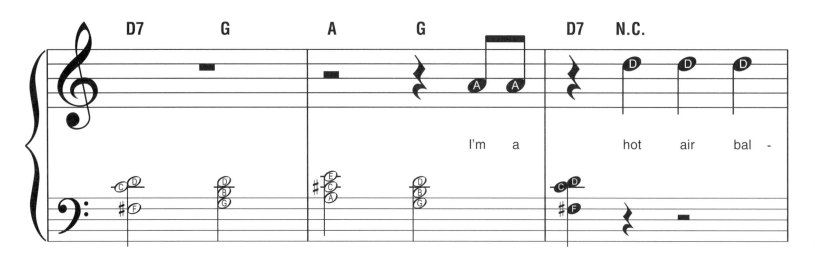

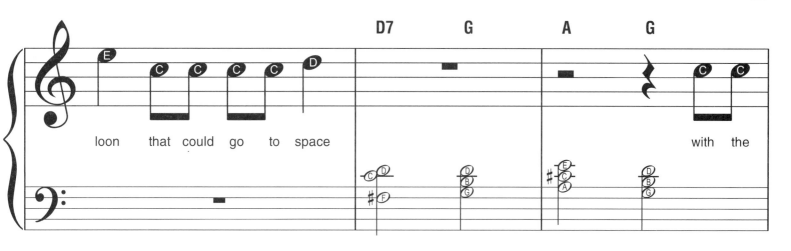

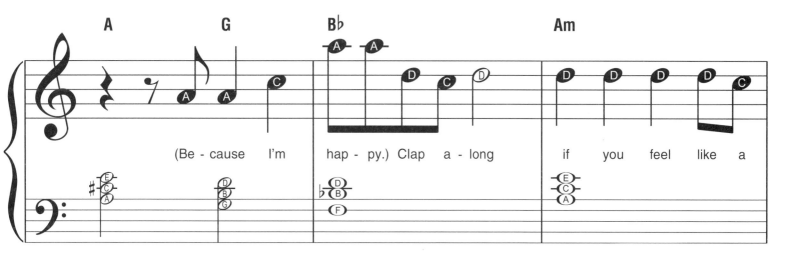

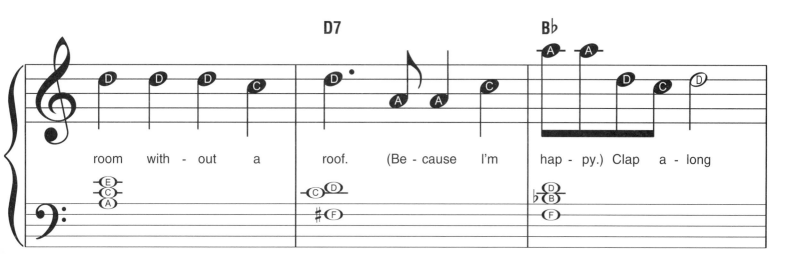

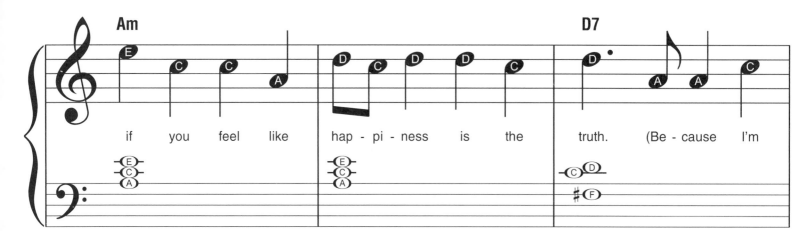

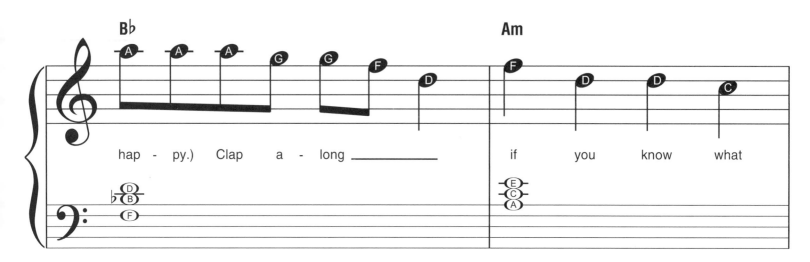

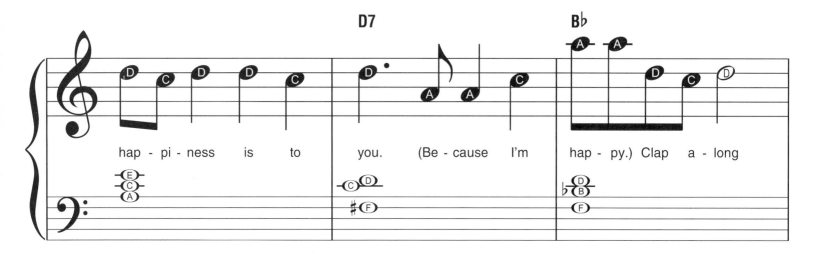

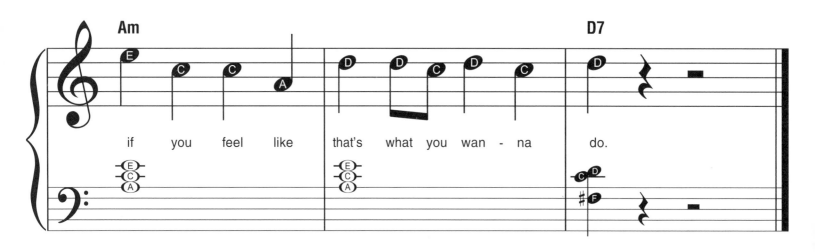

Hey, Soul Sister

Words and Music by Pat Monahan,
Espen Lind and Amund Bjorklund

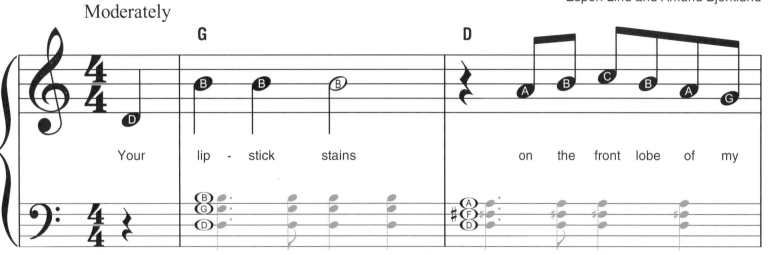

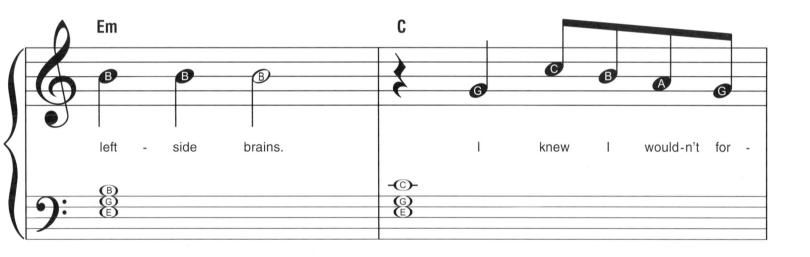

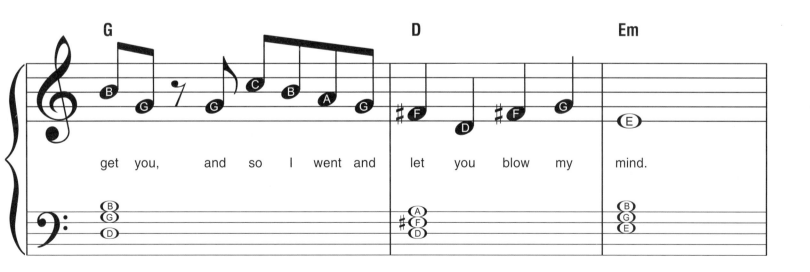

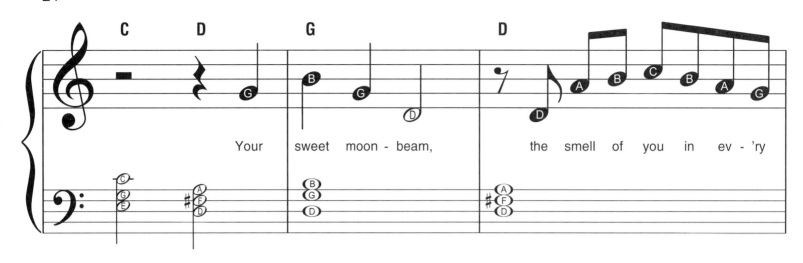

Your sweet moon - beam, the smell of you in ev - 'ry

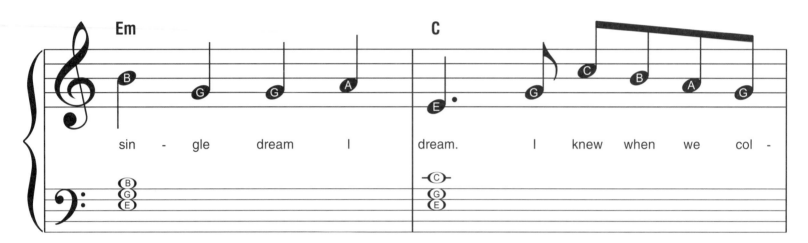

sin - gle dream I dream. I knew when we col -

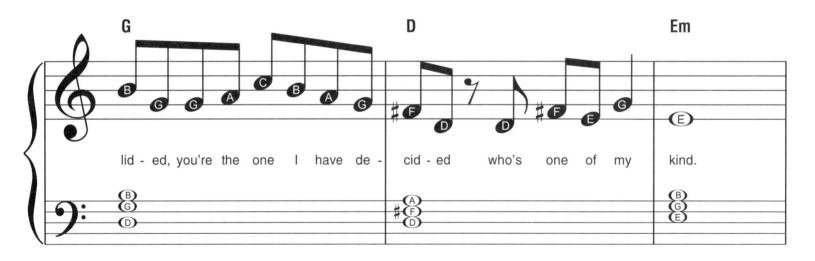

lid - ed, you're the one I have de - cid - ed who's one of my kind.

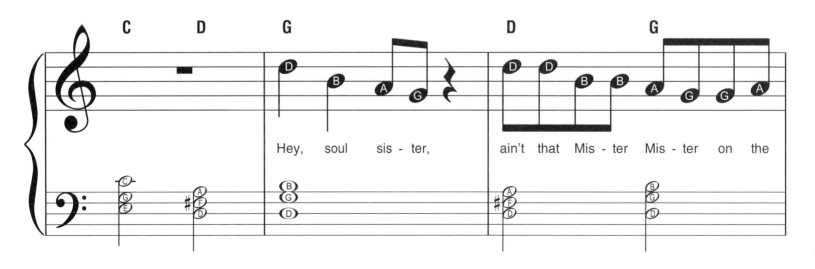

Hey, soul sis - ter, ain't that Mis - ter Mis - ter on the

Havana

Words and Music by Camila Cabello,
Louis Bell, Pharrell Williams,
Adam Feeney, Ali Tamposi, Brian Lee,
Andrew Wotman, Brittany Hazzard,
Jeffery Lamar Williams and Kaan Gunesberk

With a Latin groove

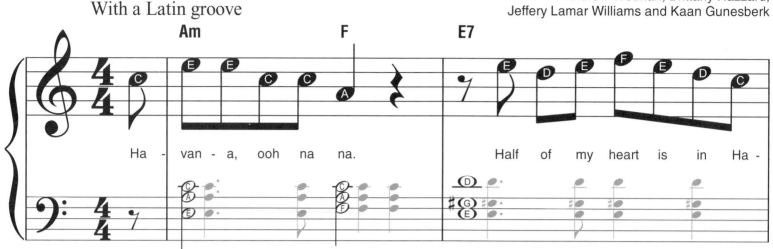

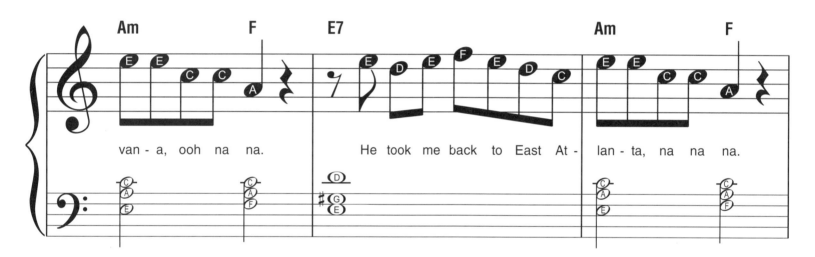

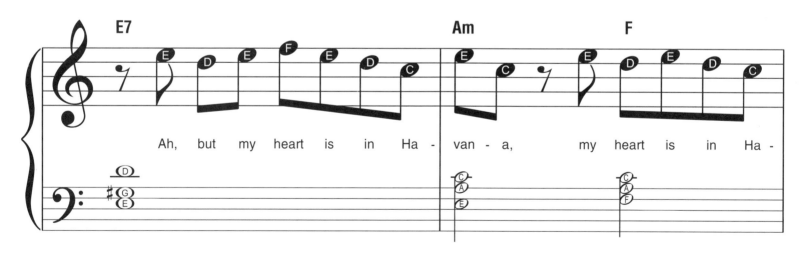

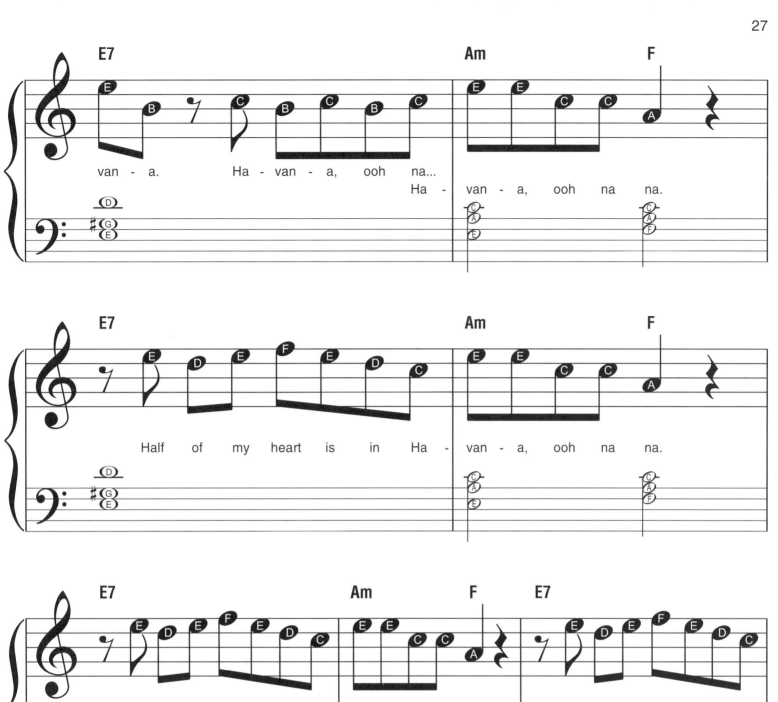

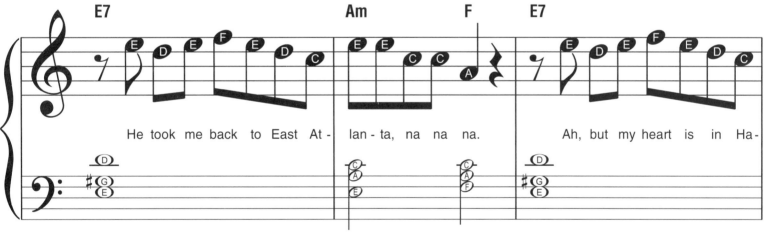

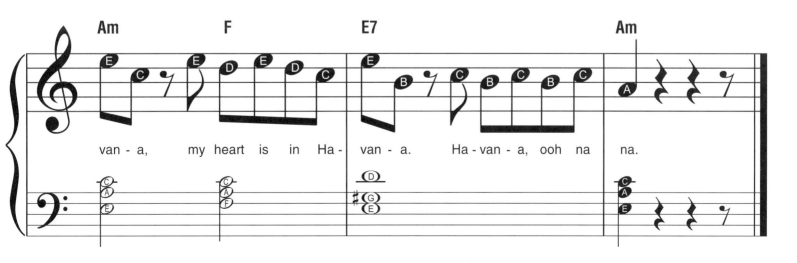

Hello

Words and Music by Adele Adkins
and Greg Kurstin

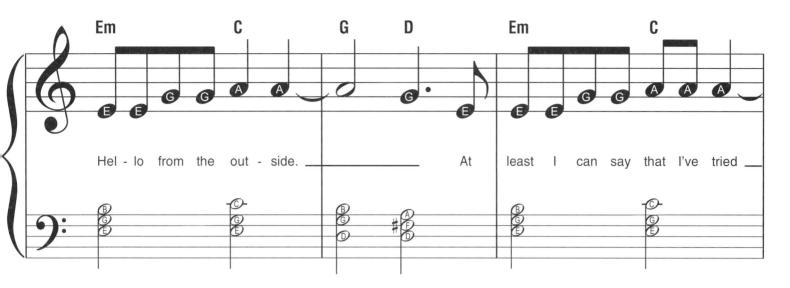

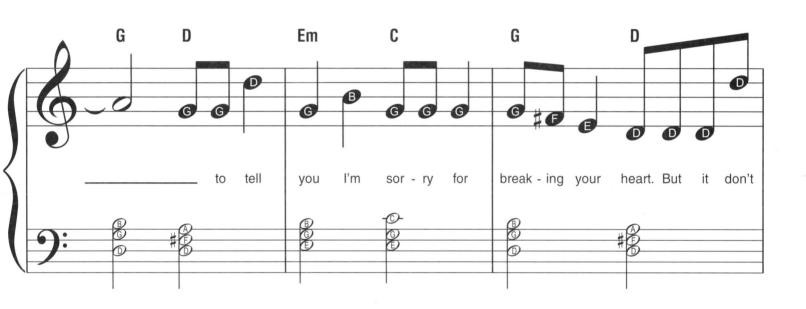

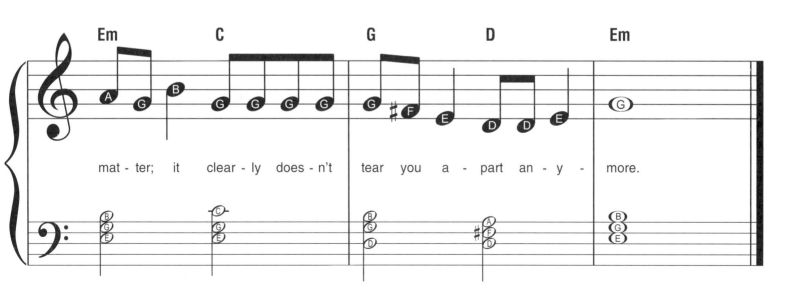

Ho Hey

Words and Music by Jeremy Fraites
and Wesley Schultz

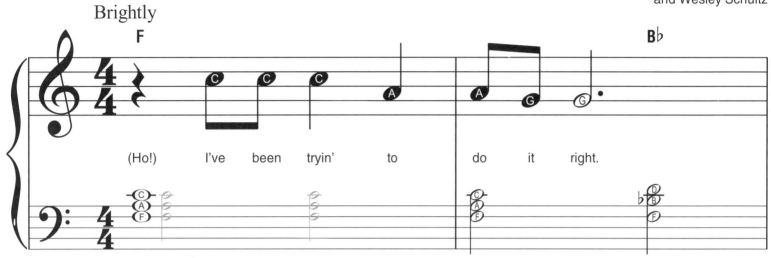

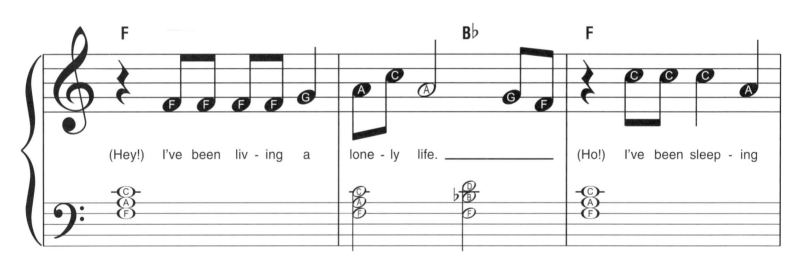

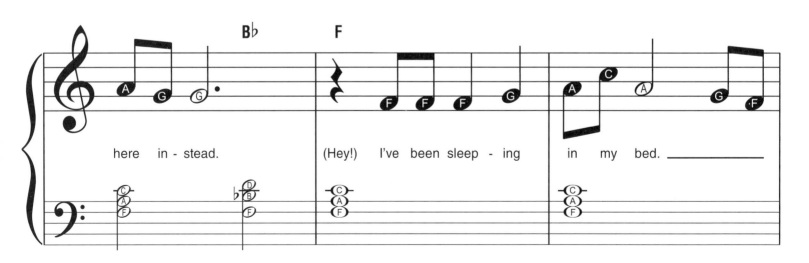

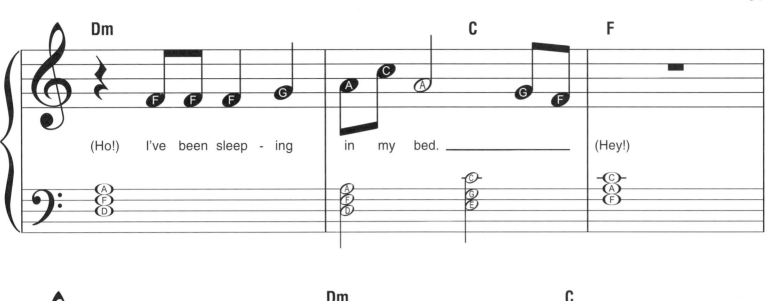

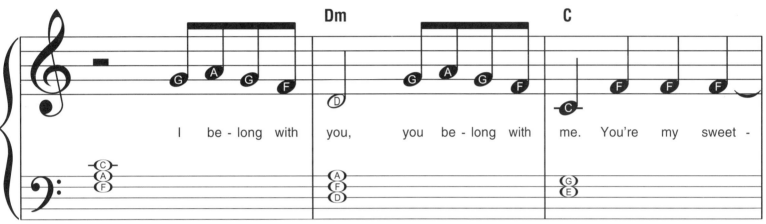

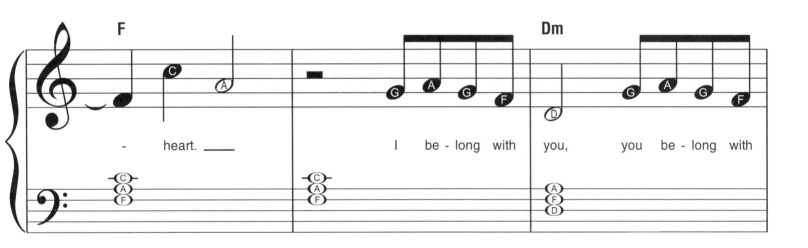

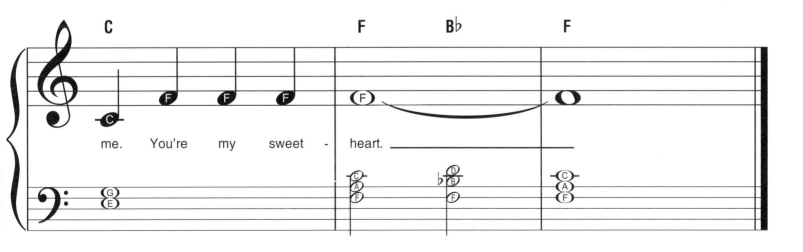

I Knew You Were Trouble

Words and Music by Taylor Swift,
Shellback and Max Martin

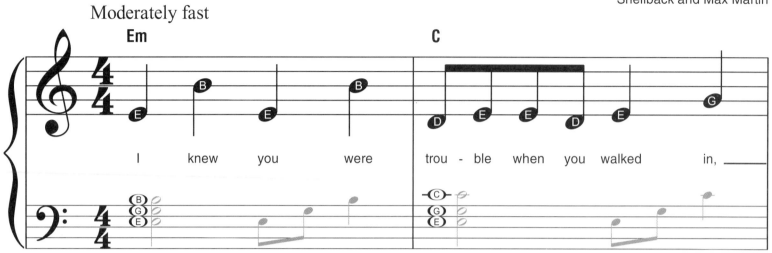

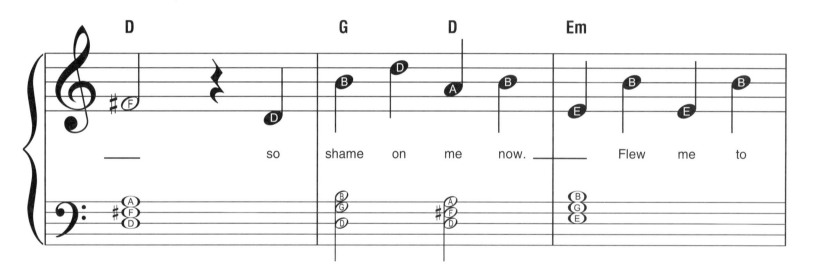

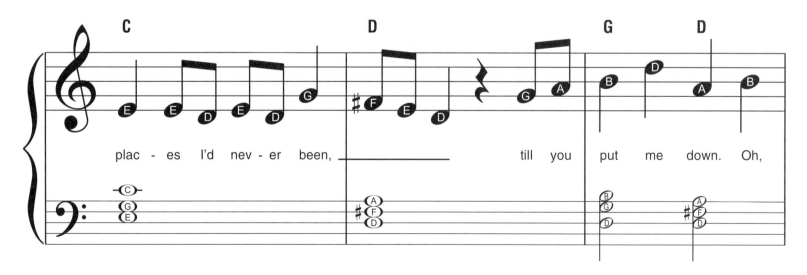

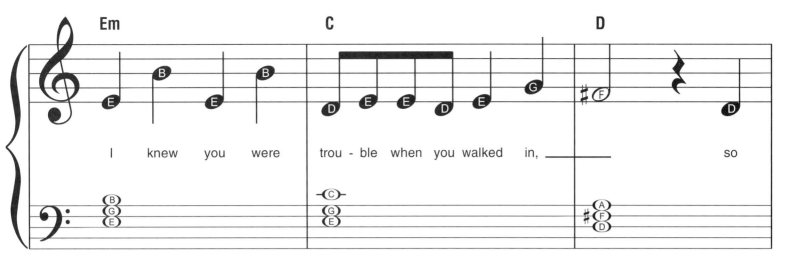

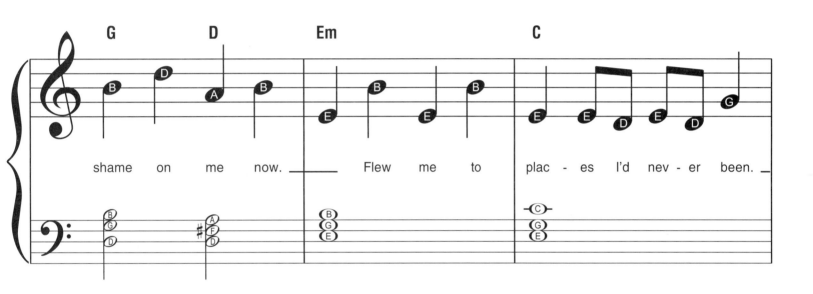

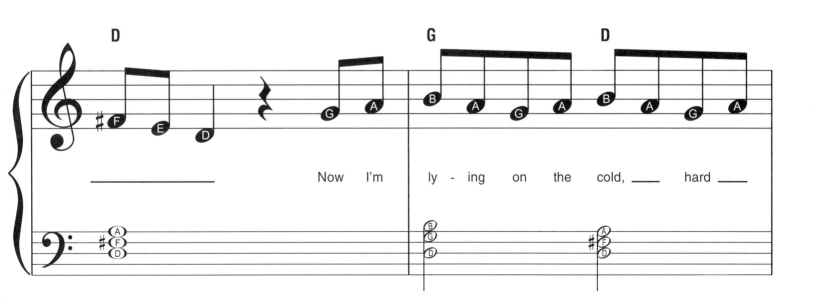

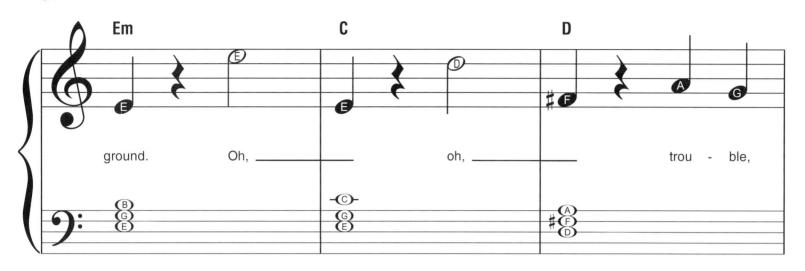

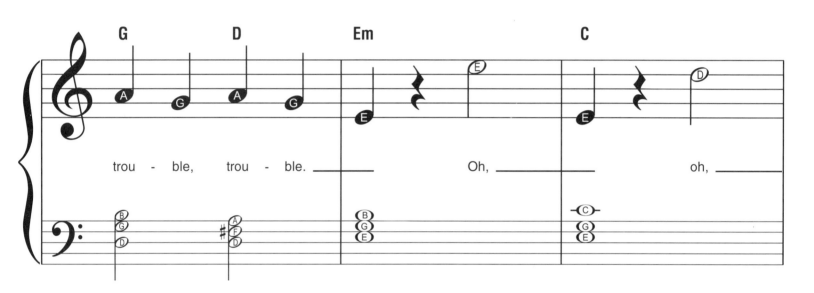

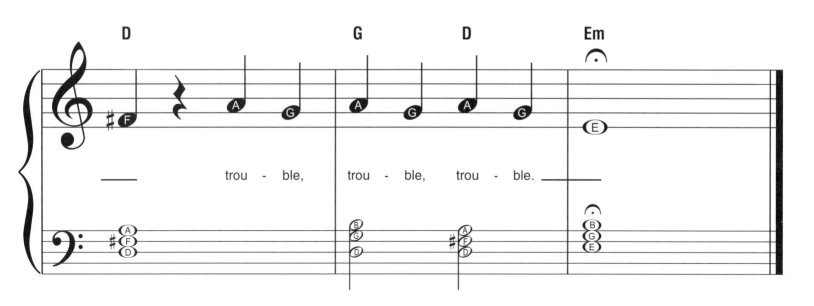

I'm Yours

Words and Music by
Jason Mraz

Moderately fast Shuffle

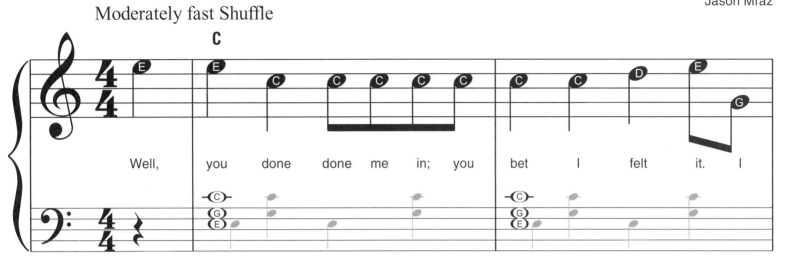

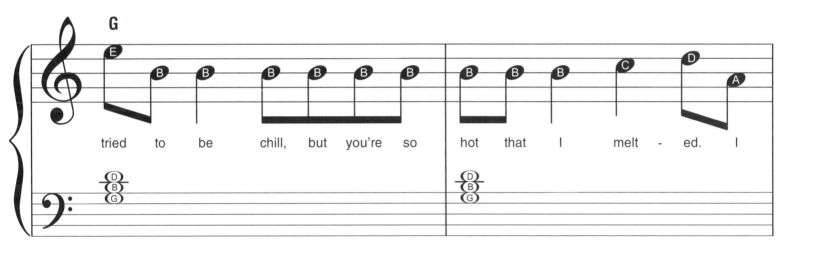

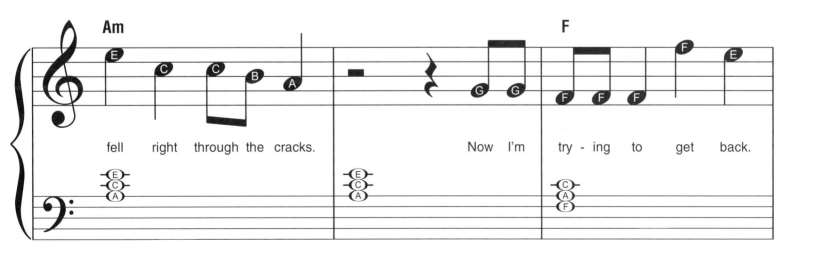

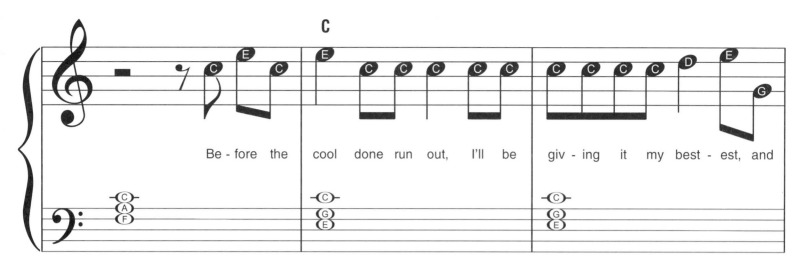

Be - fore the cool done run out, I'll be giv - ing it my best - est, and

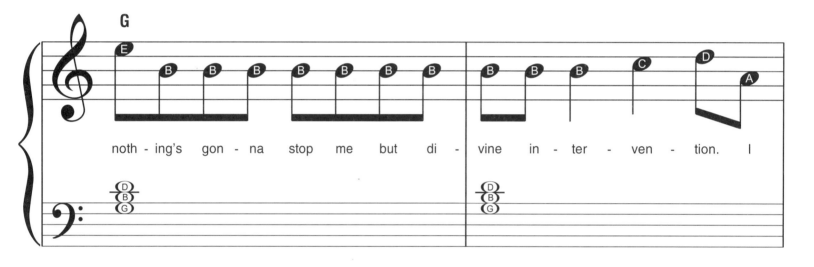

noth - ing's gon - na stop me but di - vine in - ter - ven - tion. I

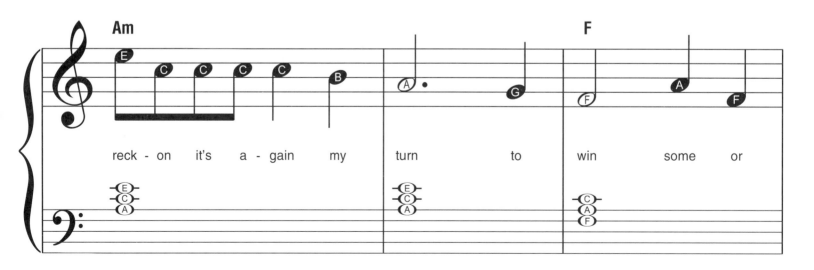

reck - on it's a - gain my turn to win some or

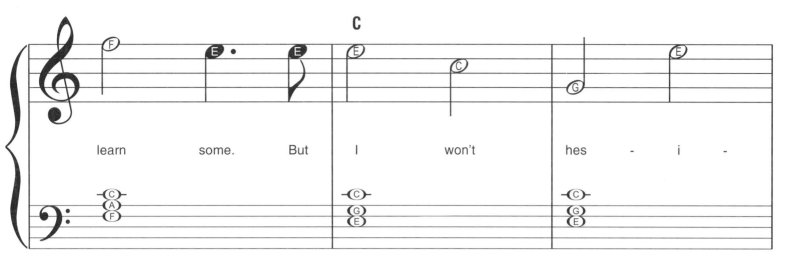

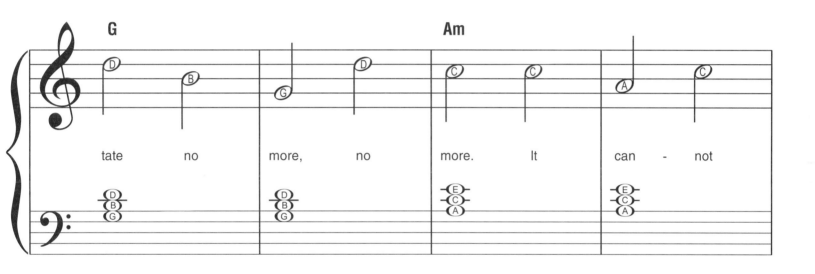

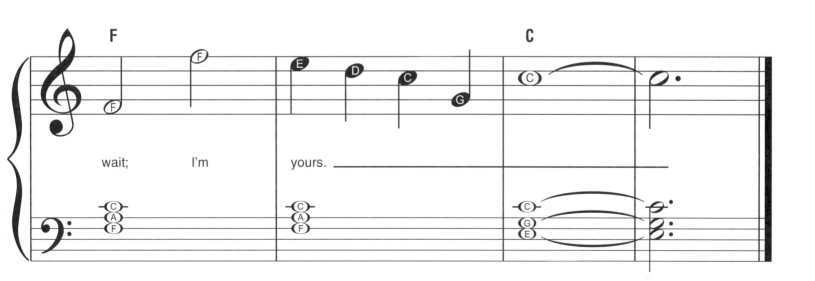

Just Give Me a Reason

Words and Music by Alecia Moore,
Jeff Bhasker and Nate Ruess

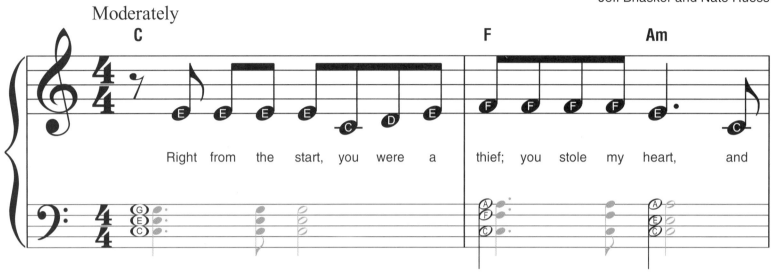

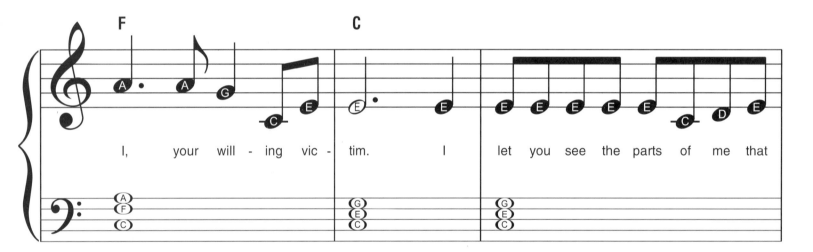

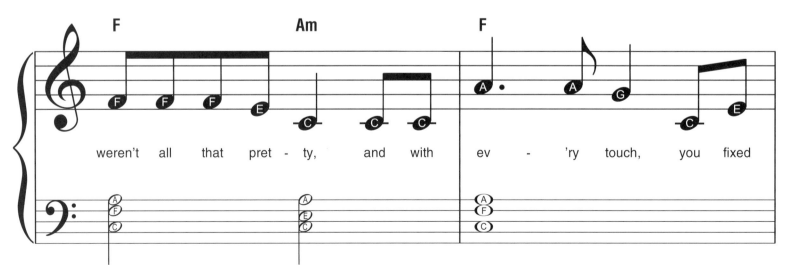

39

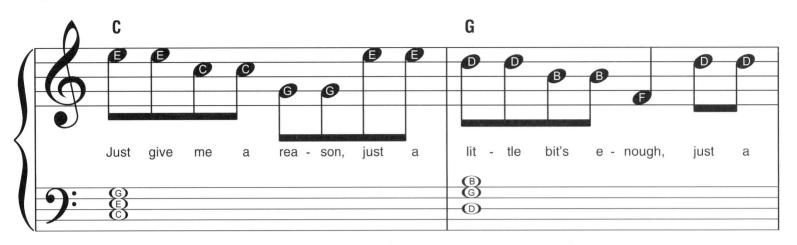

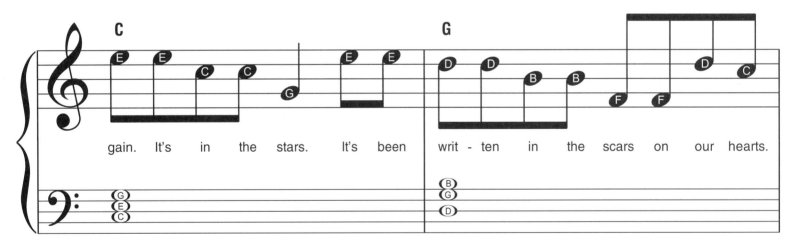

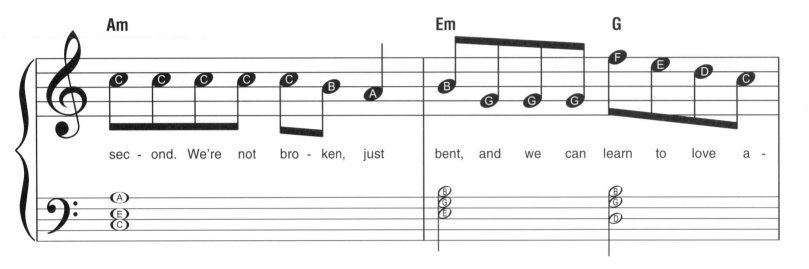

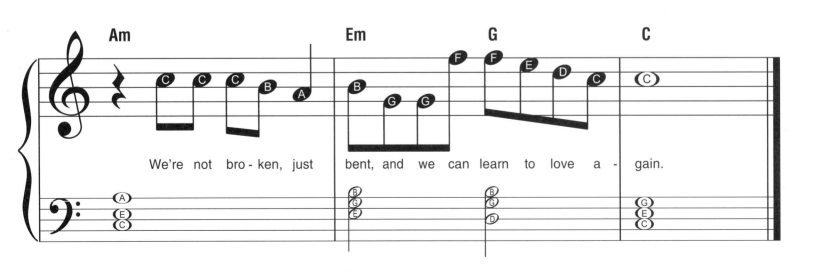

Let Her Go

Words and Music by
Michael David Rosenberg

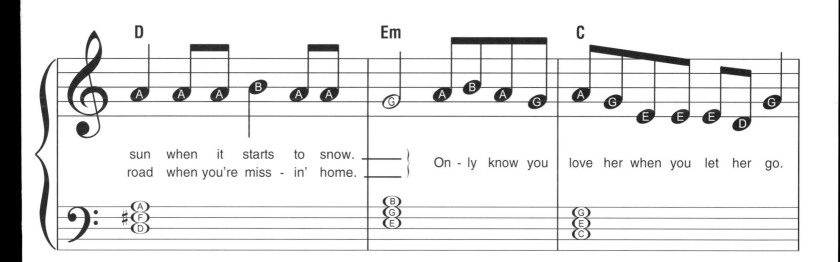

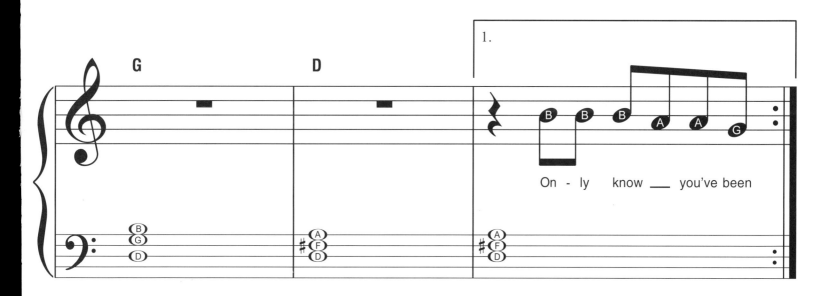

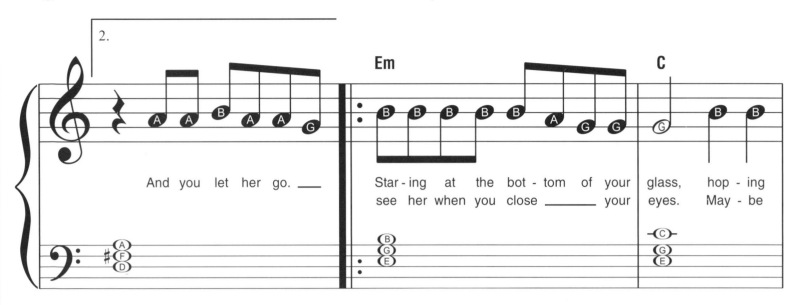

2. And you let her go. ___

Em — Star - ing at the bot - tom of your glass, hop - ing
see her when you close ___ your eyes. May - be

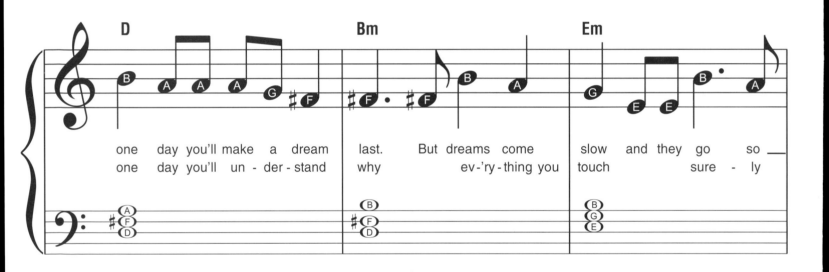

D — one day you'll make a dream
one day you'll un - der - stand

Bm — last. But dreams come
why ev - 'ry - thing you

Em — slow and they go so ___
touch sure - ly

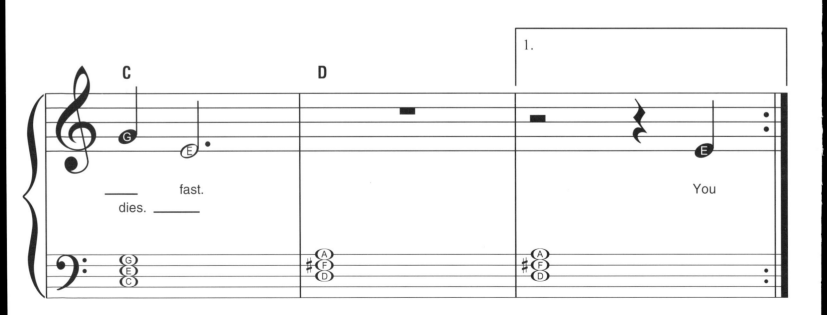

C — ___ fast.
dies. ___

D

1. You

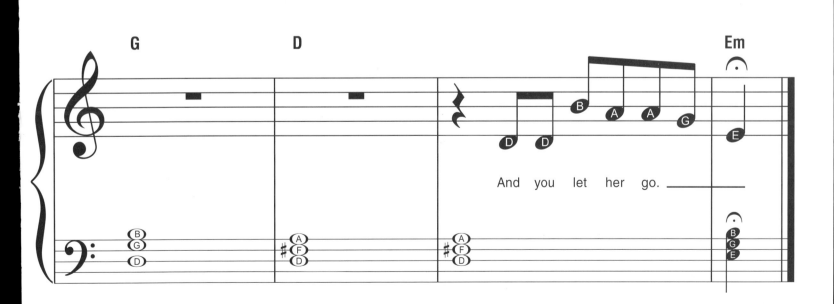

Love Yourself

Words and Music by Justin Bieber,
Benjamin Levin, Ed Sheeran,
Joshua Gudwin and Scott Braun

Lost Boy

Words and Music by
Ruth Berhe

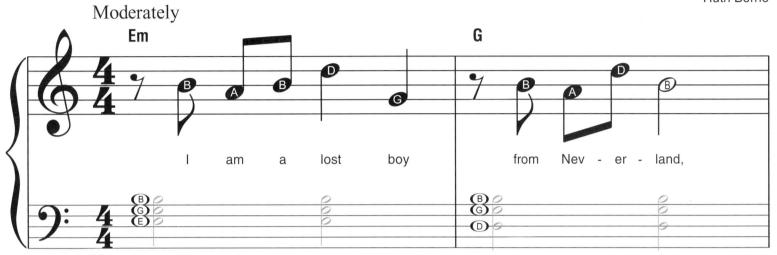

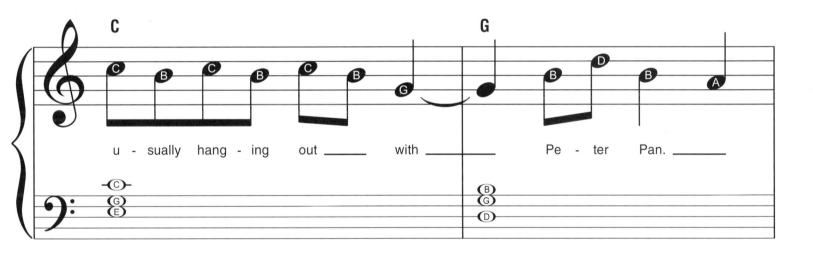

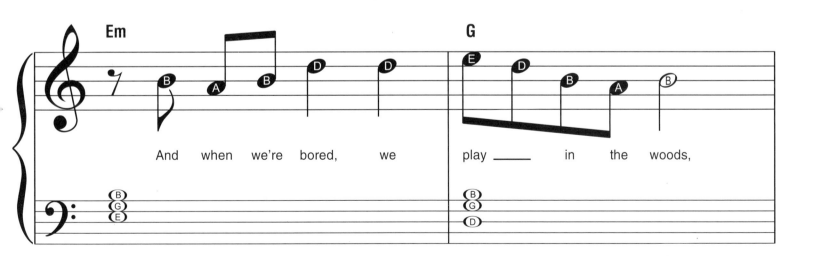

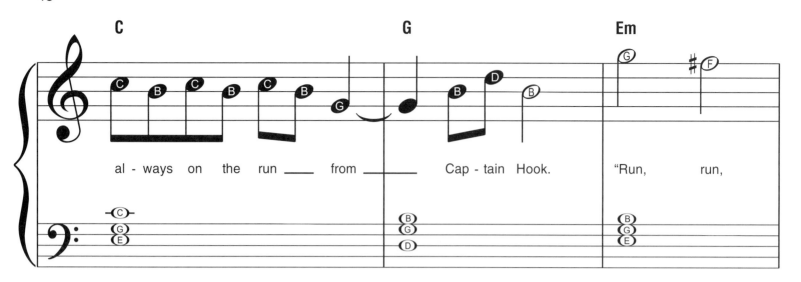

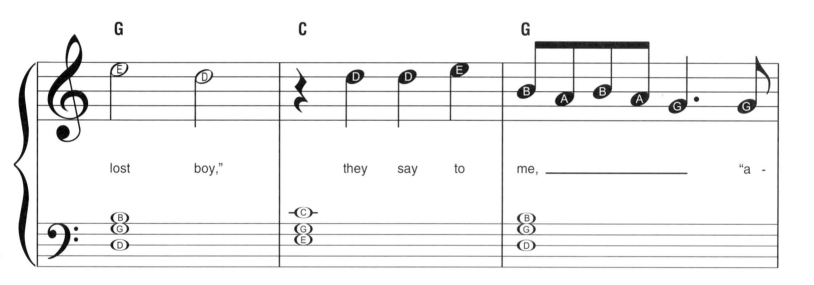

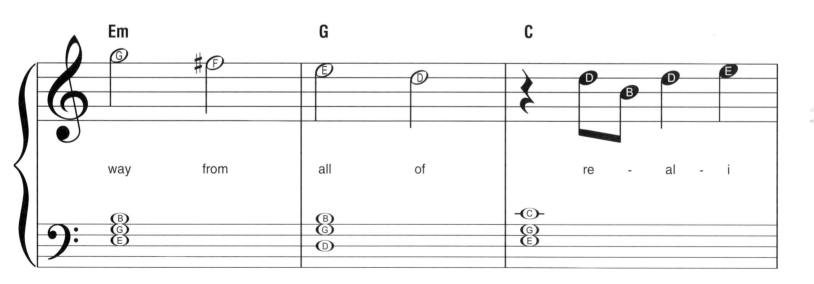

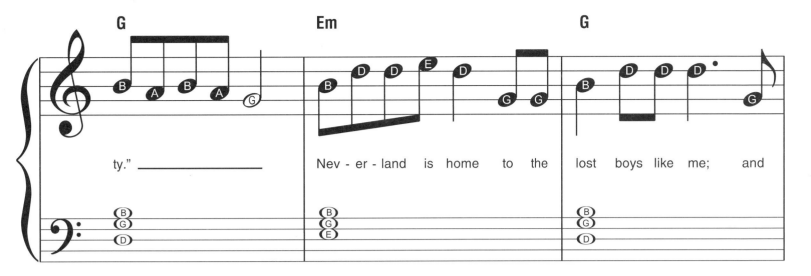

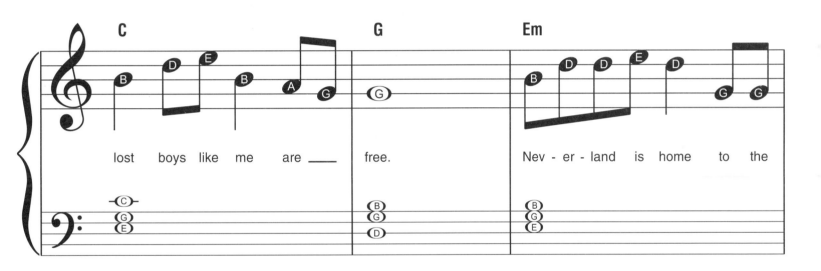

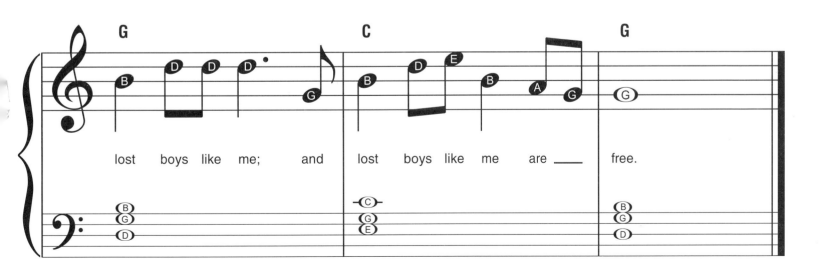

Million Reasons

Words and Music by Stefani Germanotta,
Mark Ronson and Hillary Lindsey

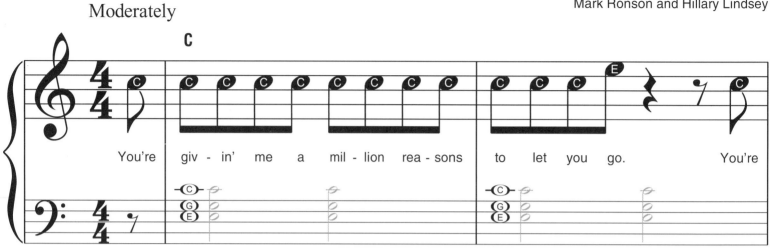

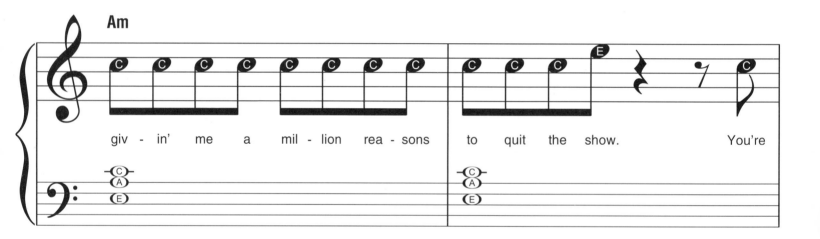

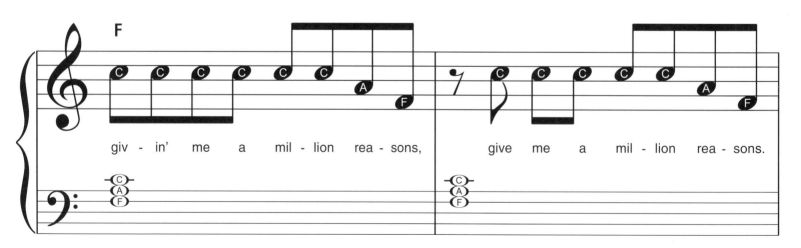

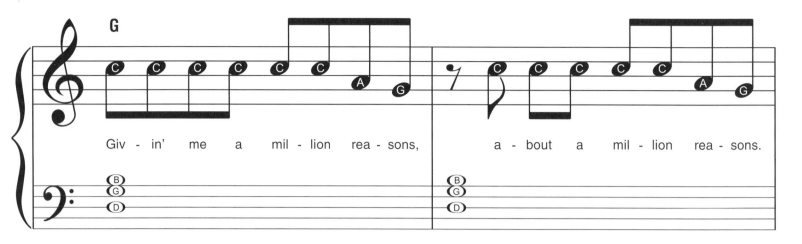

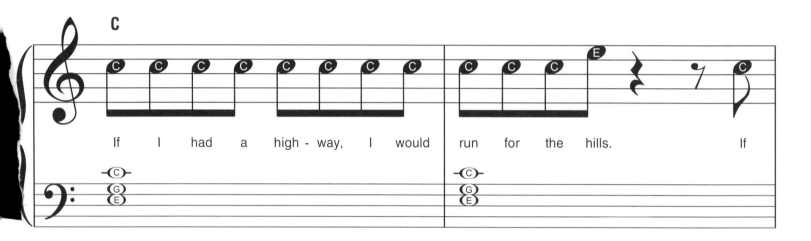

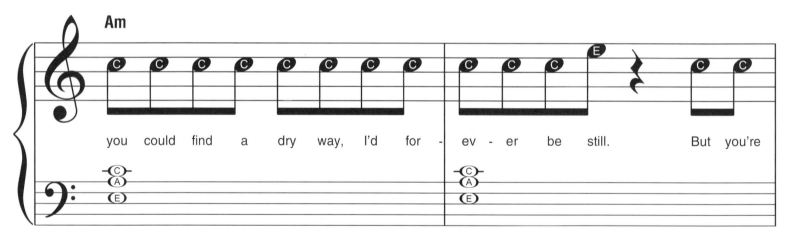

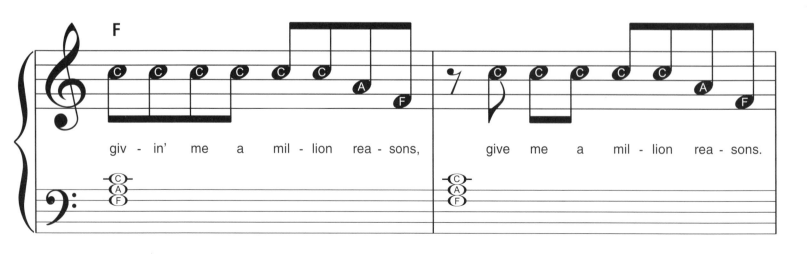

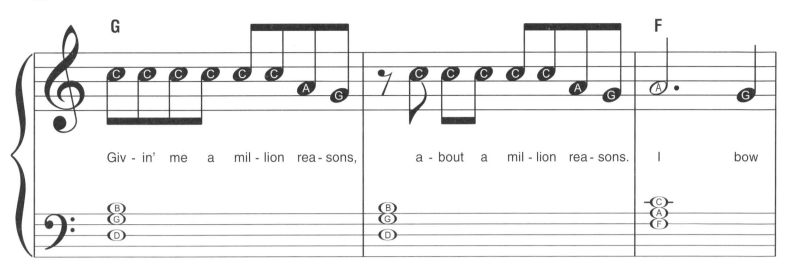

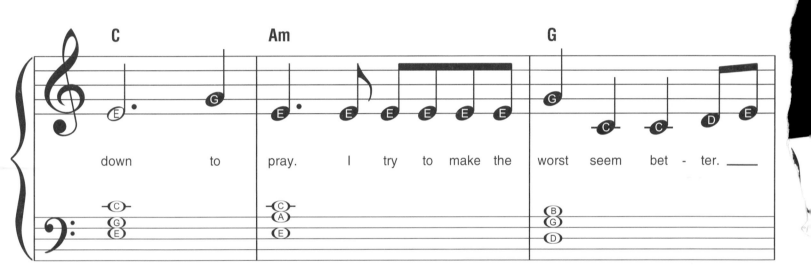

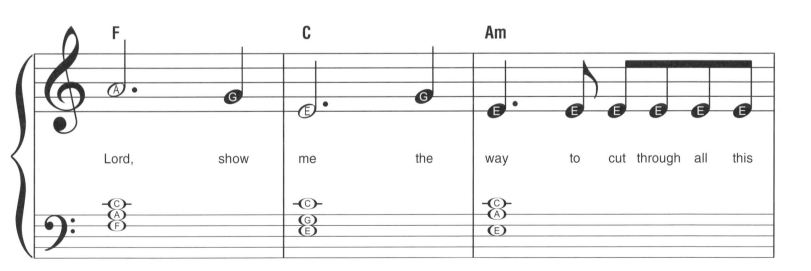

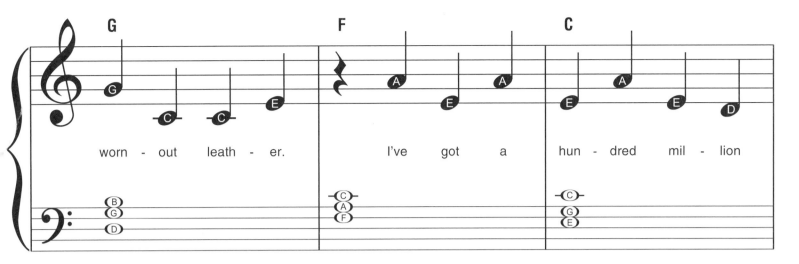

worn - out leath - er. I've got a hun - dred mil - lion

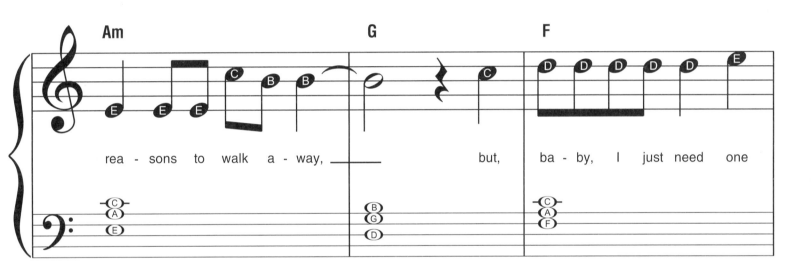

rea - sons to walk a - way, but, ba - by, I just need one

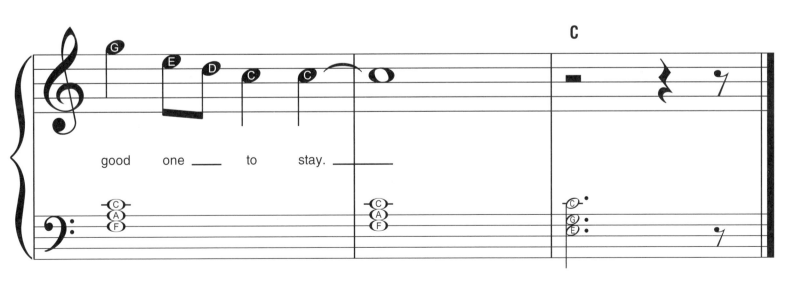

good one ___ to stay. ___

54

One Call Away

Words and Music by Charlie Puth,
Justin Franks, Breyan Isaac,
Matt Prime, Blake Anthony Carter
and Maureen McDonald

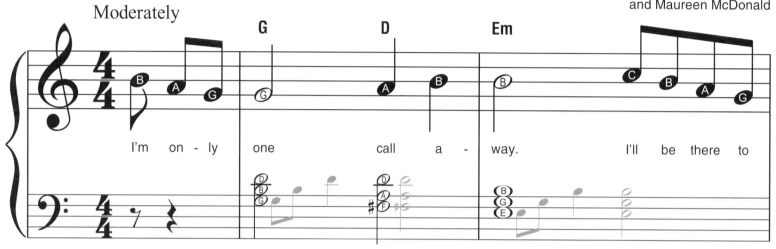

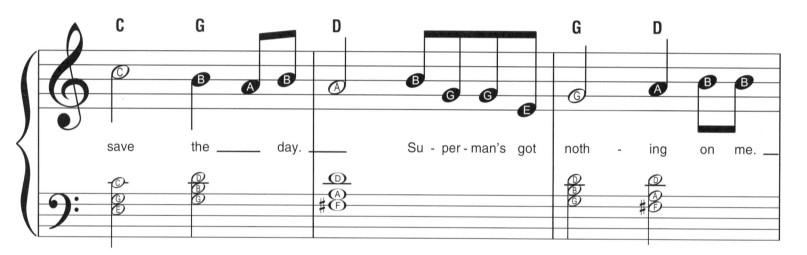

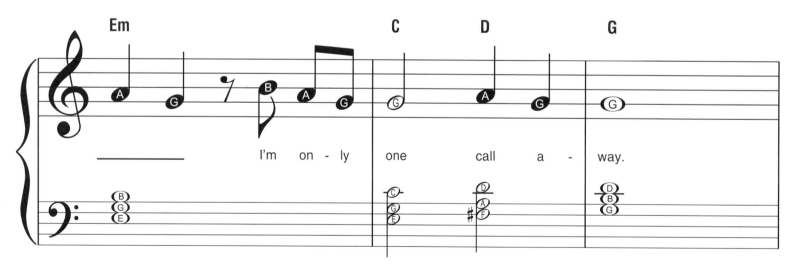

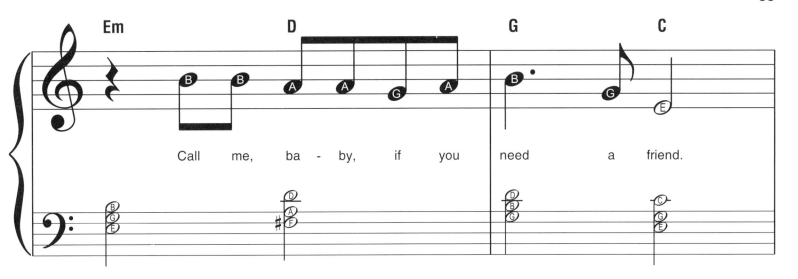

Call me, ba - by, if you need a friend.

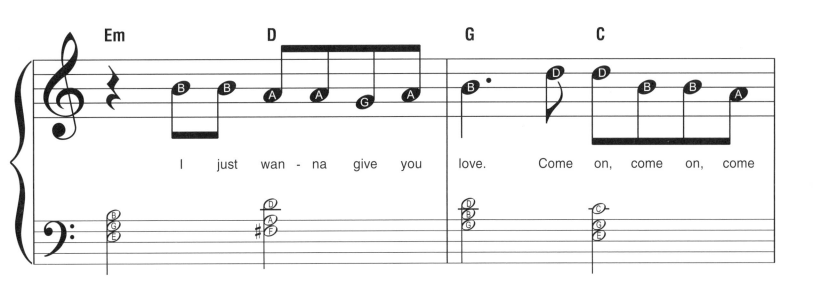

I just wan - na give you love. Come on, come on, come

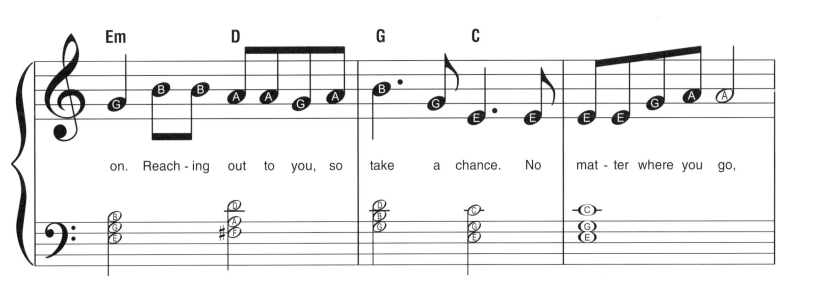

on. Reach - ing out to you, so take a chance. No mat - ter where you go,

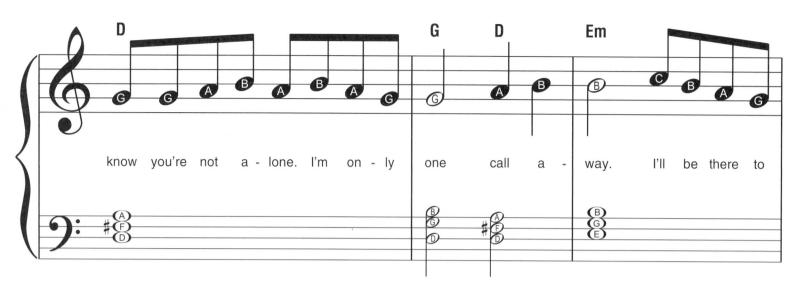

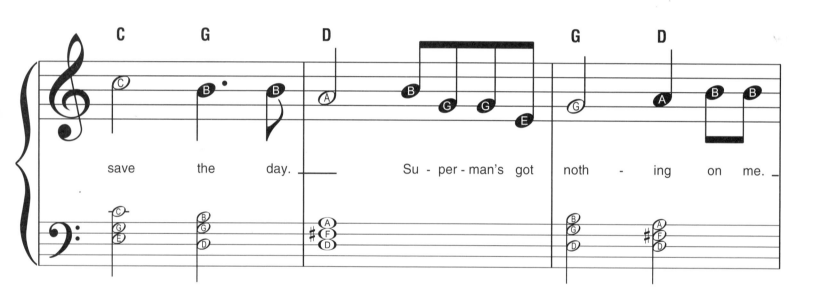

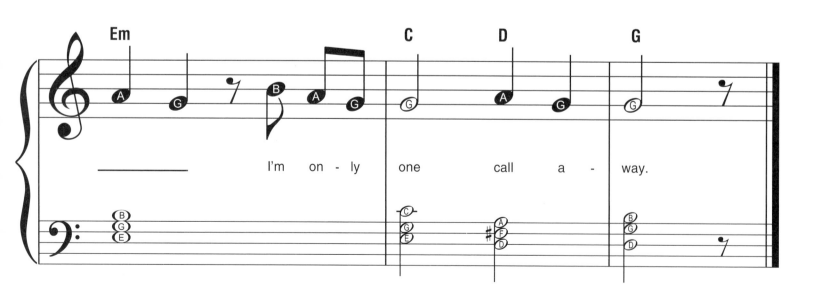

100 Years

Words and Music by
John Ondrasik

Moderately fast

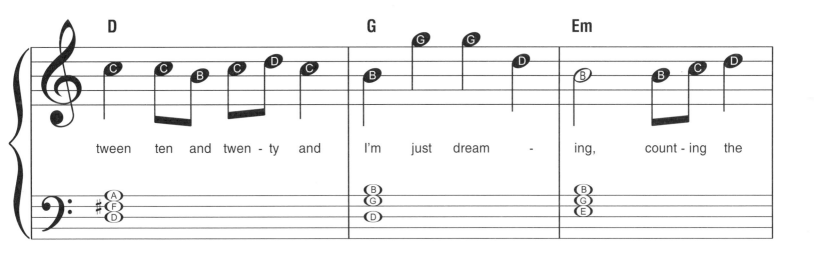

I'm fif - teen ____ for a mo - ment, caught in be -

tween ten and twen - ty and I'm just dream - ing, count - ing the

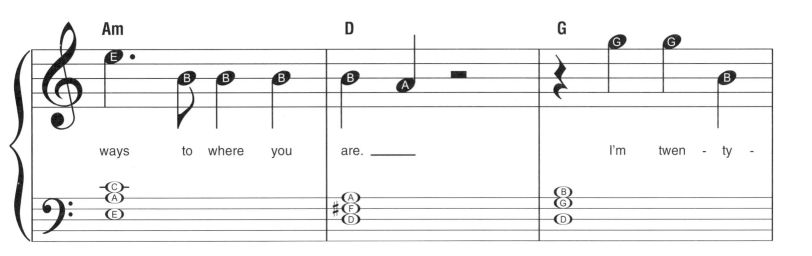

ways to where you are. ____ I'm twen - ty -

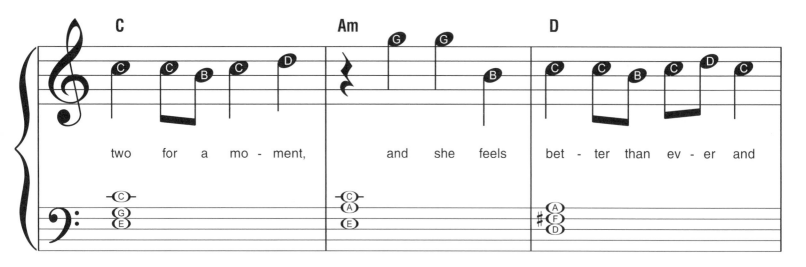

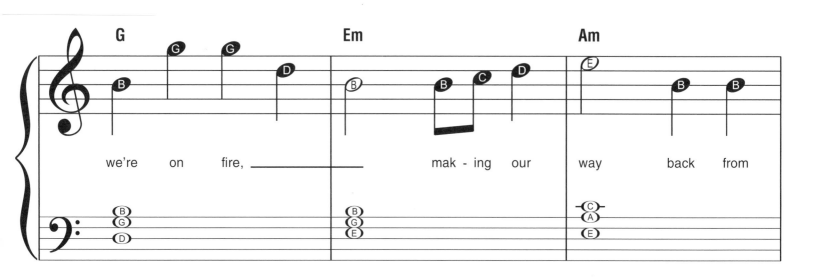

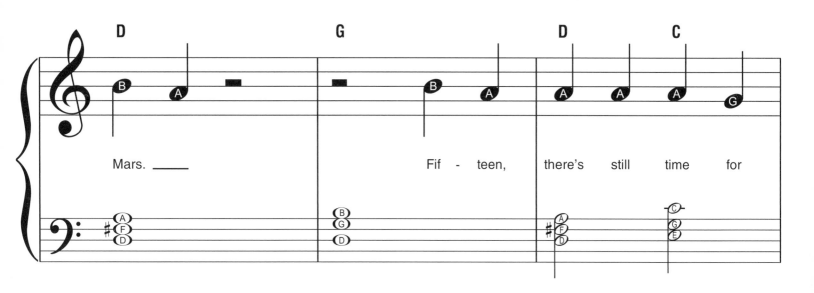

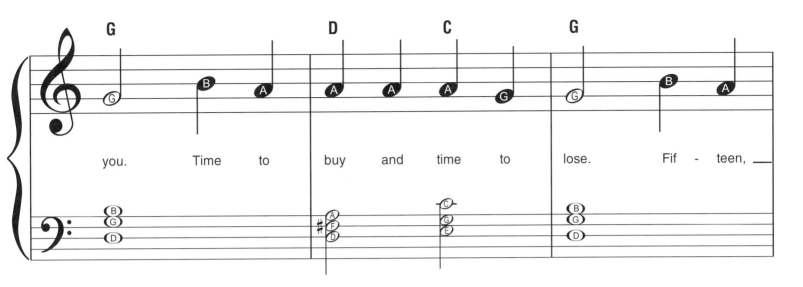

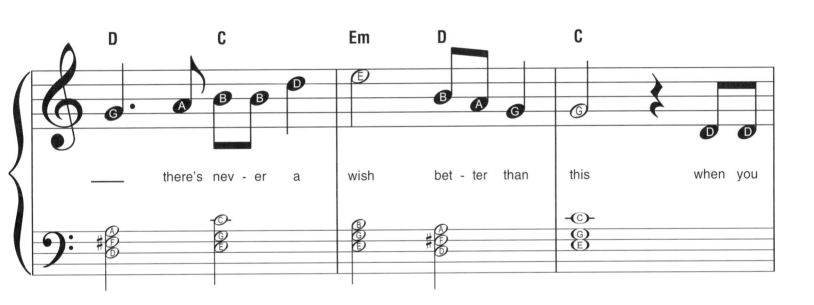

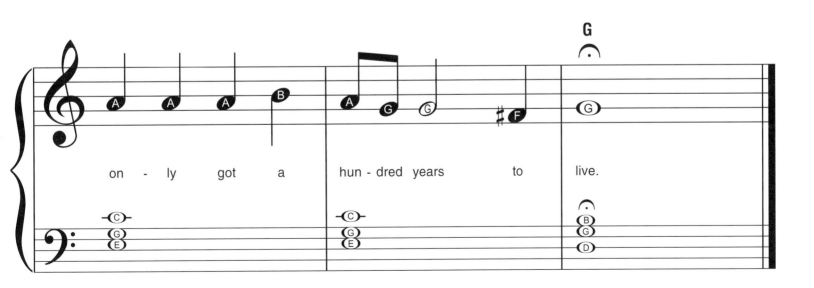

Perfect

Words and Music by
Ed Sheeran

Say You Won't Let Go

Words and Music by Steven Solomon,
James Arthur and Neil Ormandy

Moderate Ballad

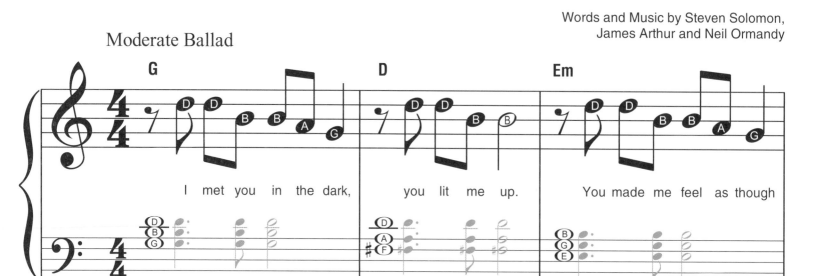

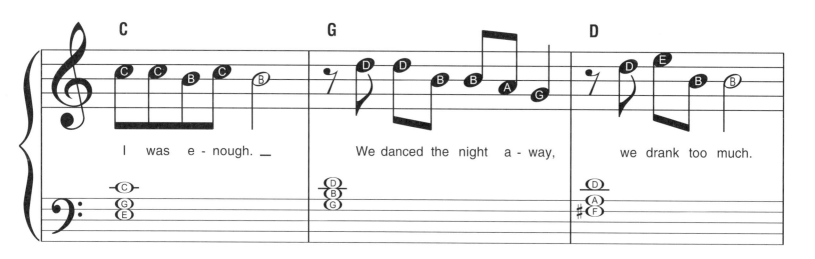

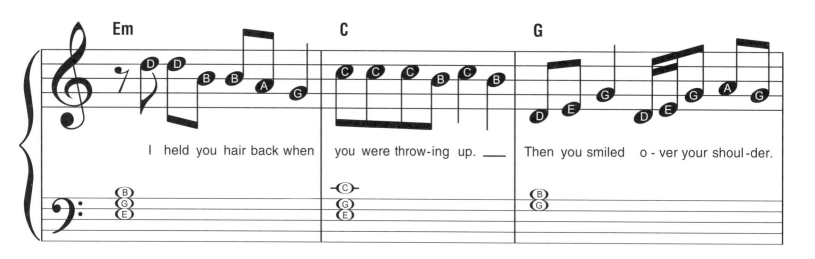

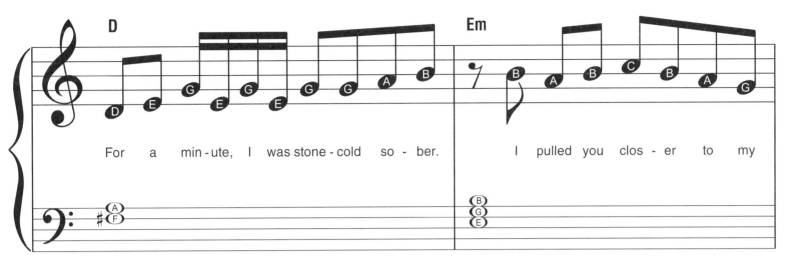

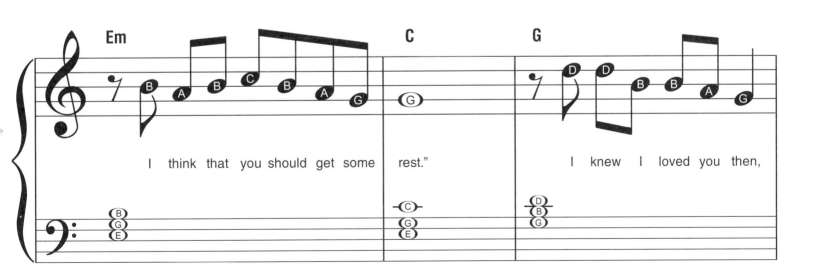

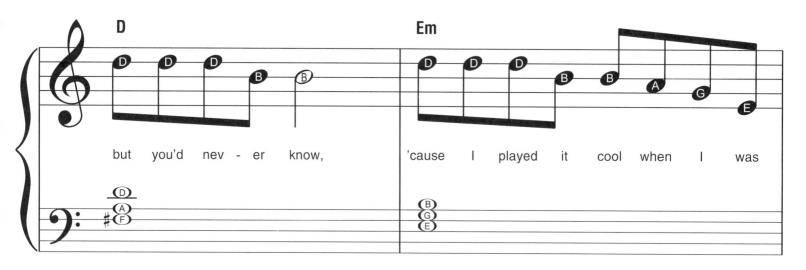

but you'd nev - er know, 'cause I played it cool when I was

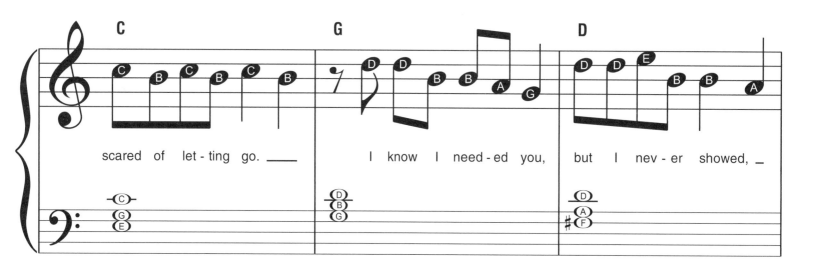

scared of let - ting go. ____ I know I need - ed you, but I nev - er showed, _

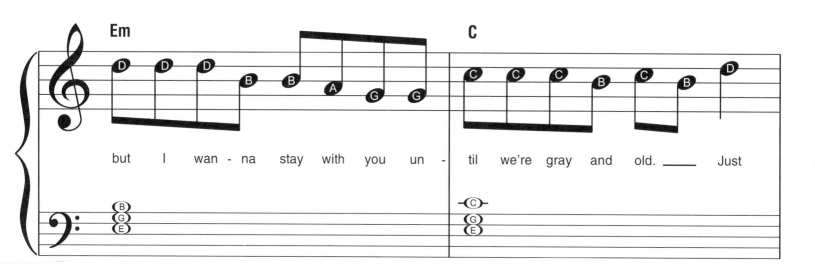

but I wan - na stay with you un - til we're gray and old. ____ Just

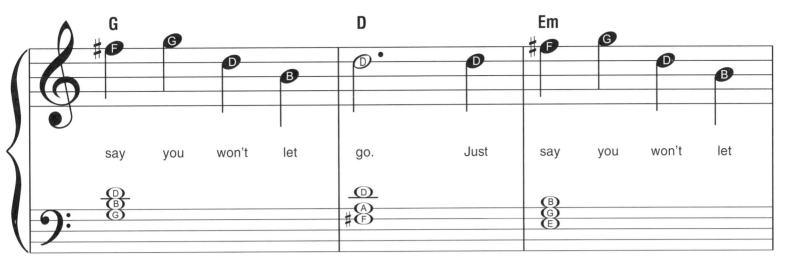

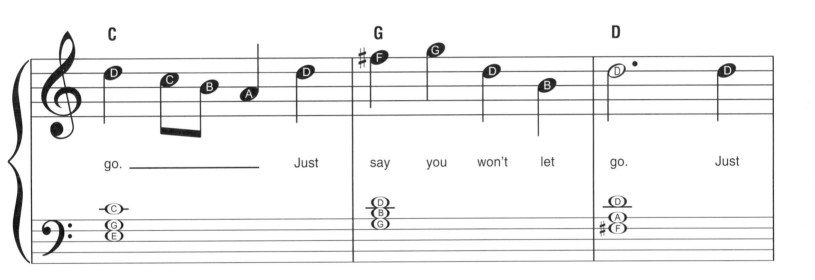

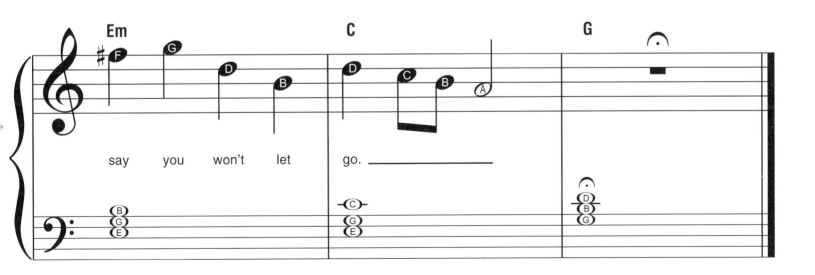

See You Again

from FURIOUS 7

Words and Music by Cameron Thomaz,
Charlie Puth, Justin Franks,
Andrew Cedar, Dann Hume,
Josh Hardy and Phoebe Cockburn

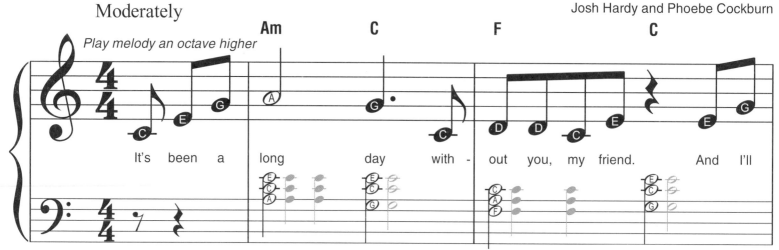

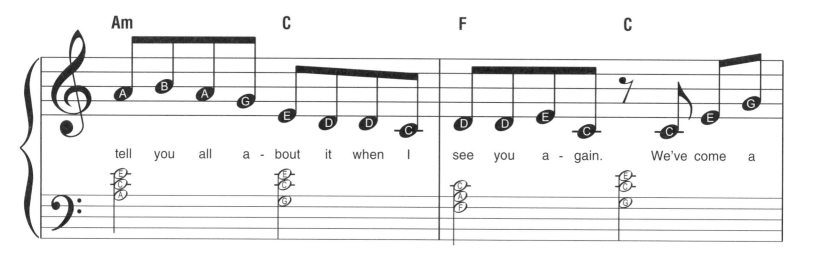

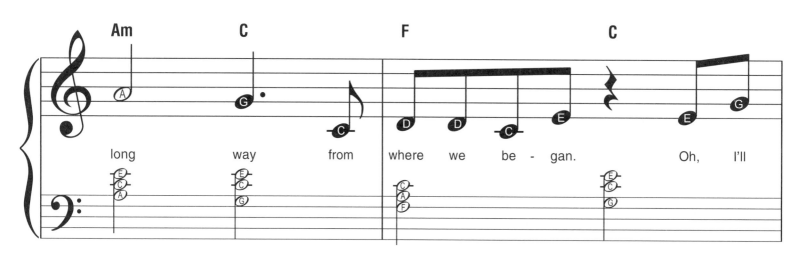

7 Years

Words and Music by Lukas Forchhammer,
Morten Ristorp, Stefan Forrest,
David Labrel, Christopher Brown
and Morten Pilegaard

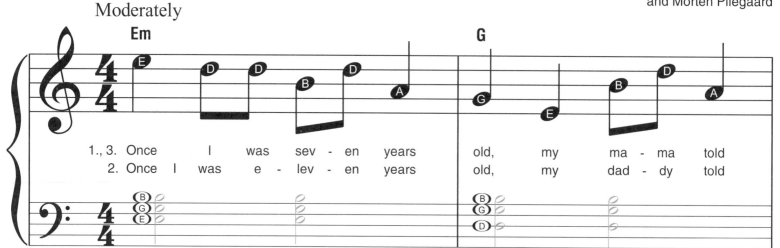

1., 3. Once I was sev - en years old, my ma - ma told
2. Once I was e - lev - en years old, my dad - dy told

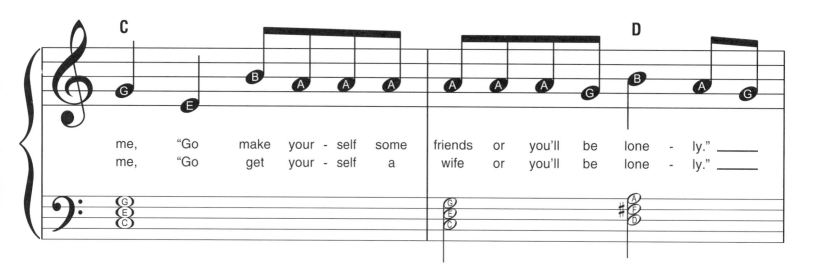

me, "Go make your - self some friends or you'll be lone - ly." ____
me, "Go get your - self a wife or you'll be lone - ly." ____

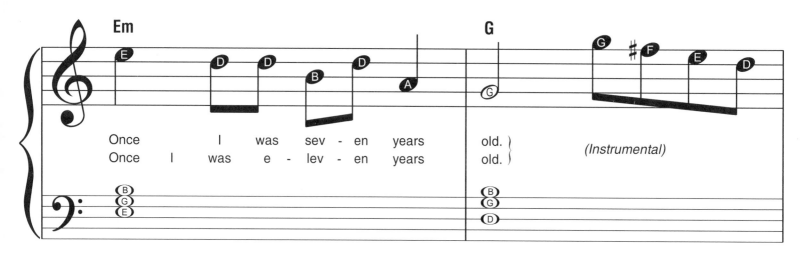

Once I was sev - en years old. }
Once I was e - lev - en years old. }   (Instrumental)

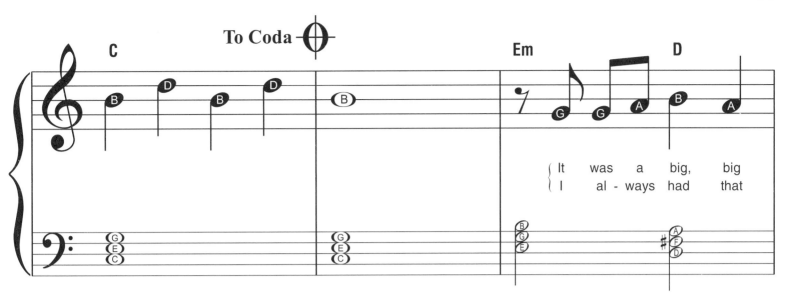

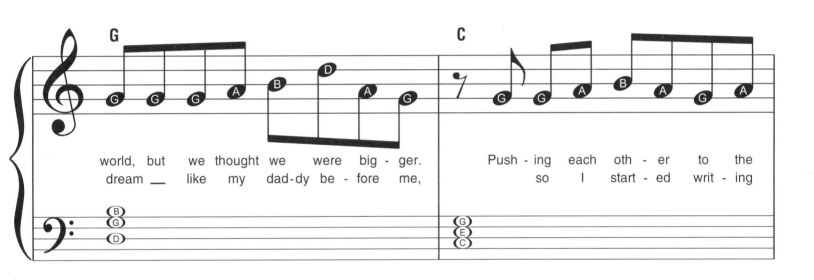

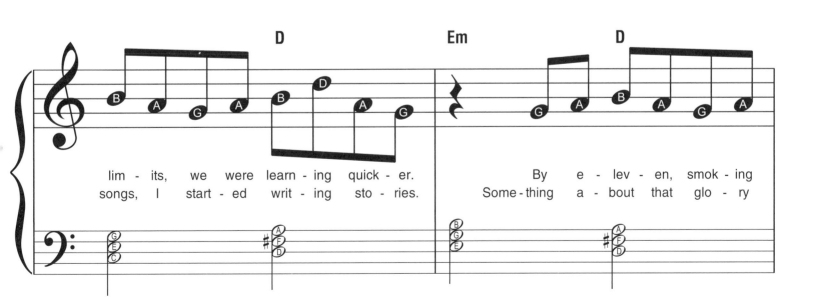

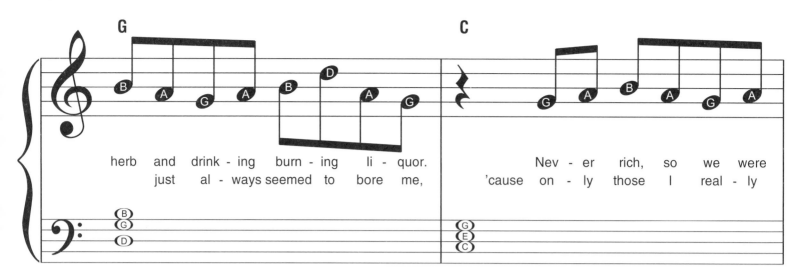

herb and drink - ing burn - ing li - quor.
just al - ways seemed to bore me,

Nev - er rich, so we were
'cause on - ly those I real - ly

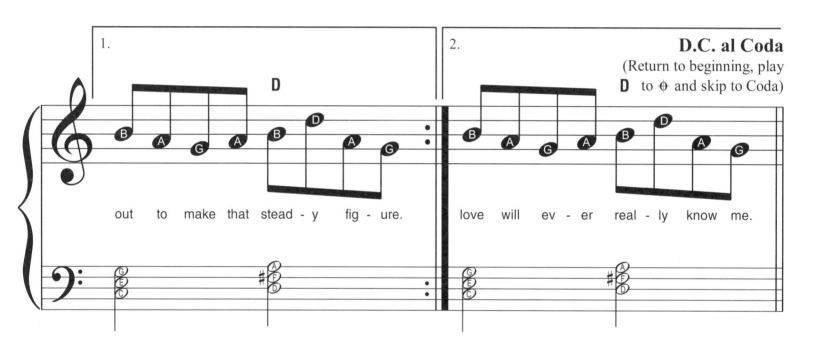

D.C. al Coda
(Return to beginning, play
D to ⊕ and skip to Coda)

out to make that stead - y fig - ure.

love will ev - er real - ly know me.

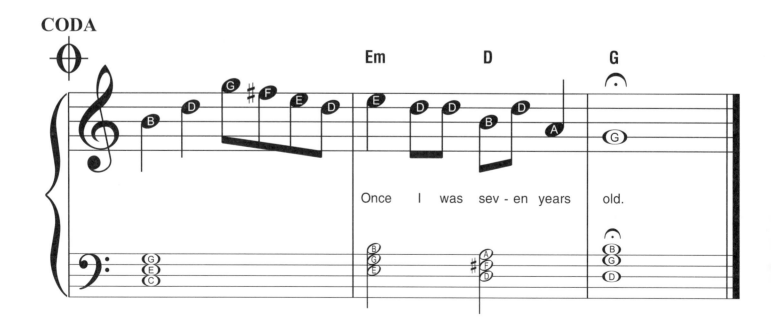

CODA

Once I was sev - en years old.

Riptide

Words and Music by
Vance Joy

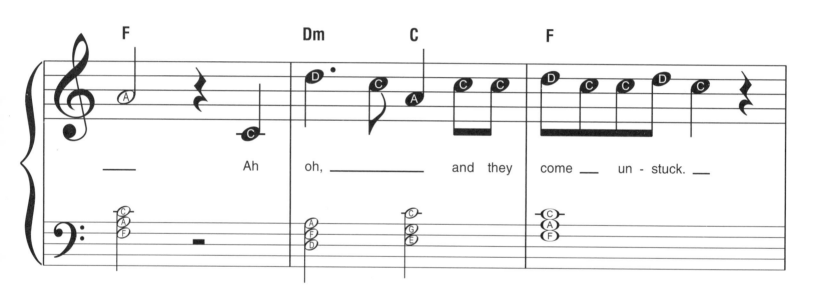

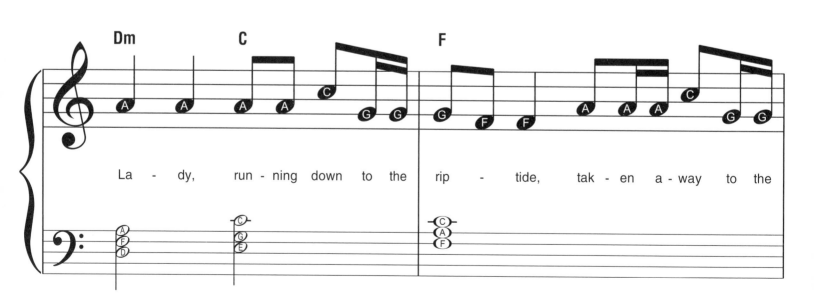

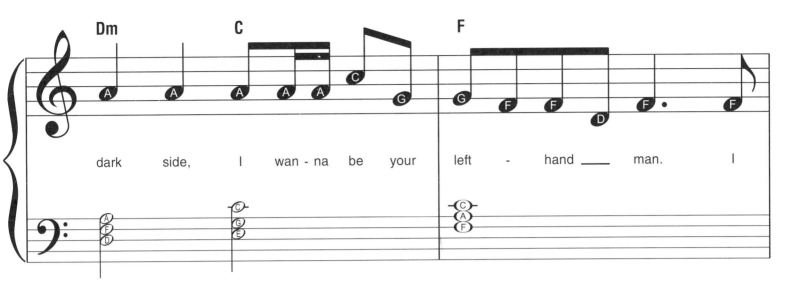

Shake It Off

Words and Music by Taylor Swift,
Max Martin and Shellback

Moderately fast

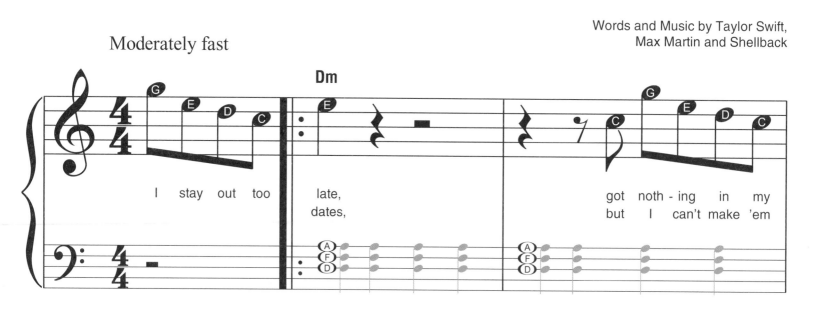

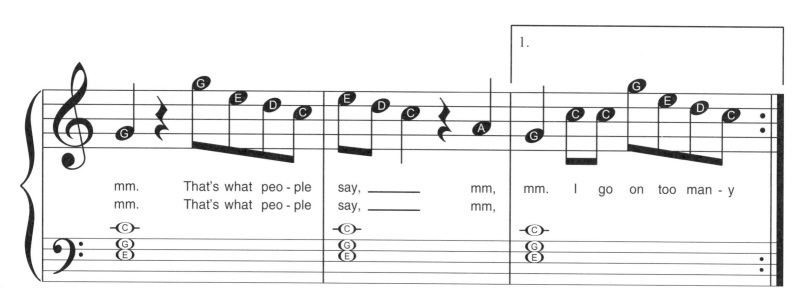

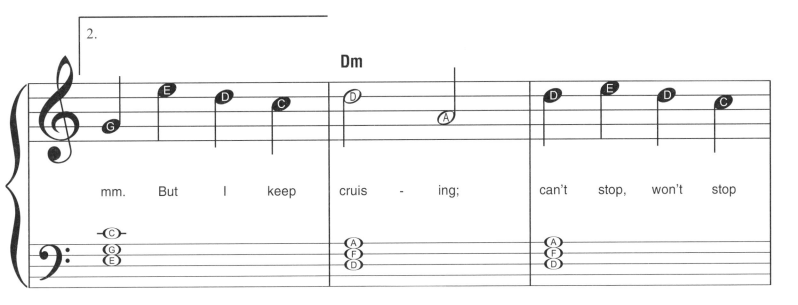

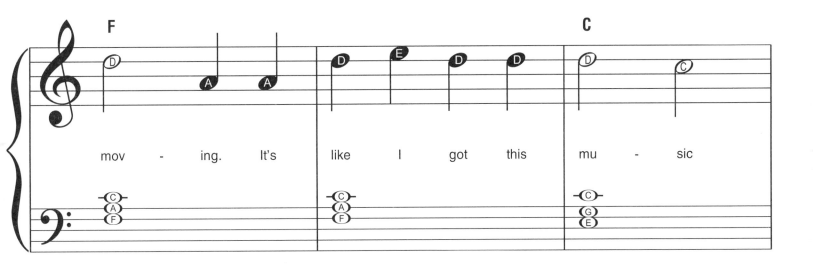

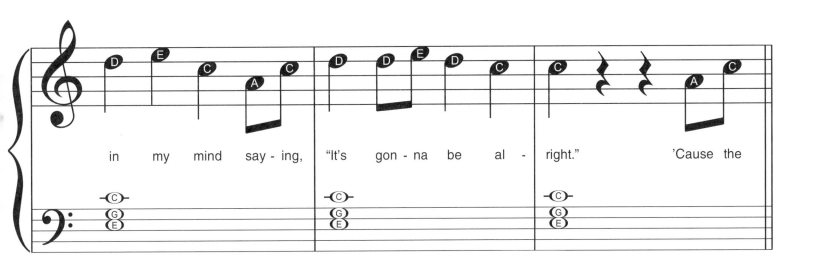

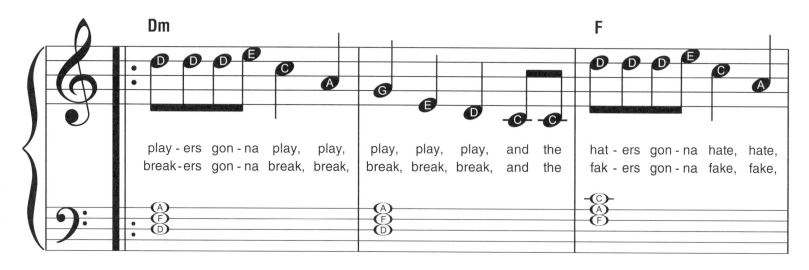

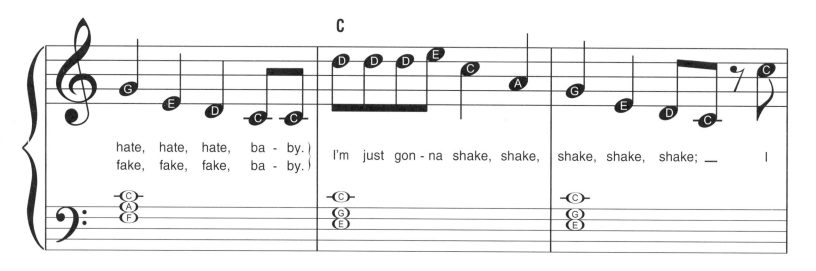

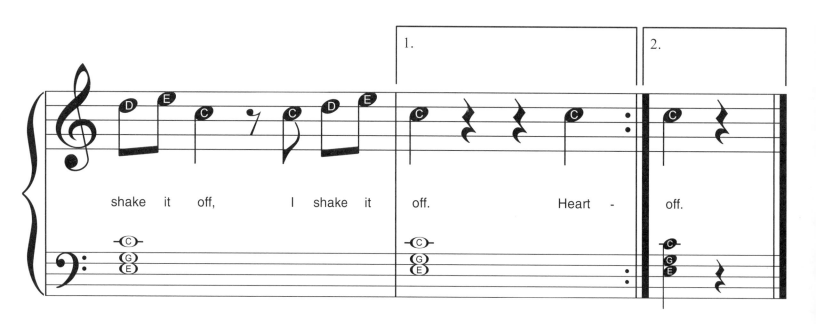

Viva La Vida

Words and Music by Guy Berryman,
Jon Buckland, Will Champion
and Chris Martin

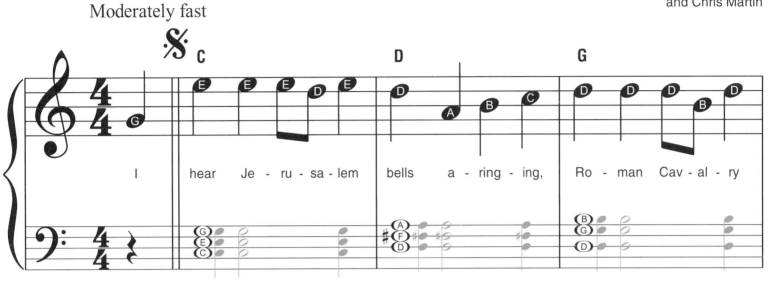

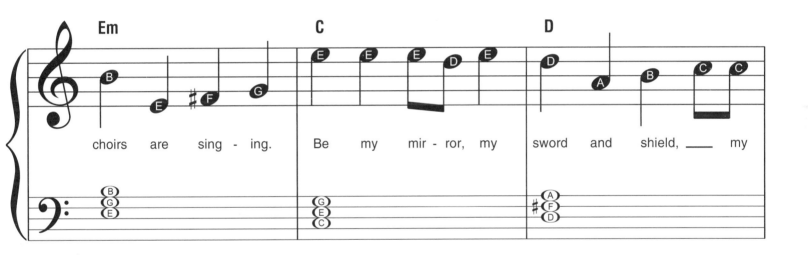

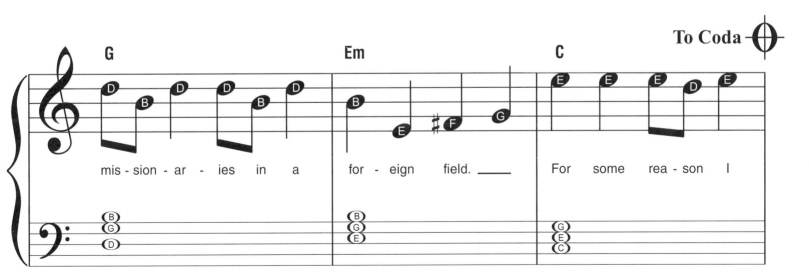

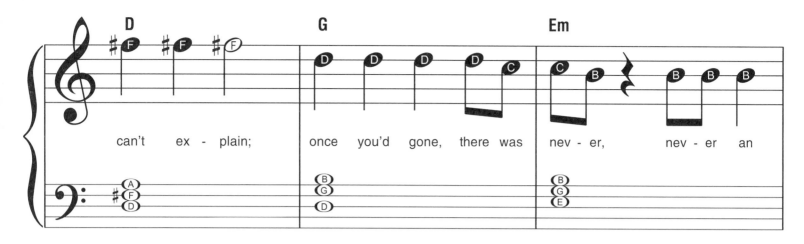

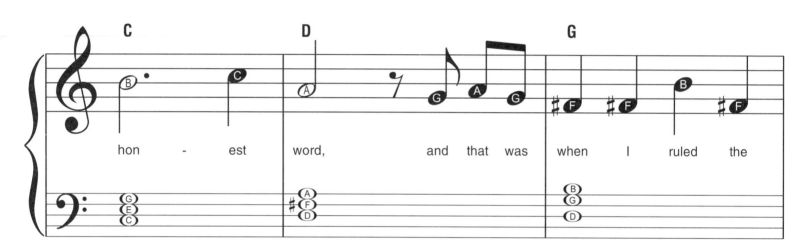

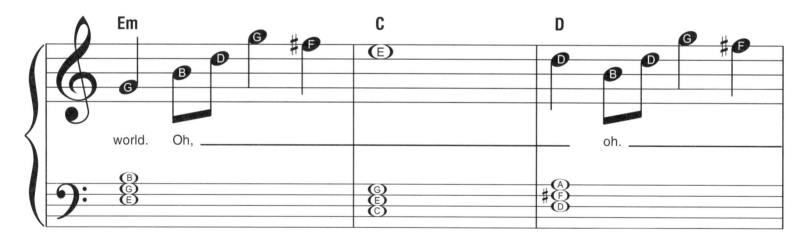

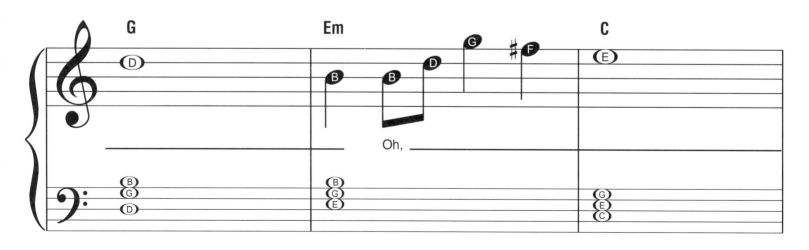

D.S. al Coda
(Return to 𝄋, play to ✛
and skip to Coda)

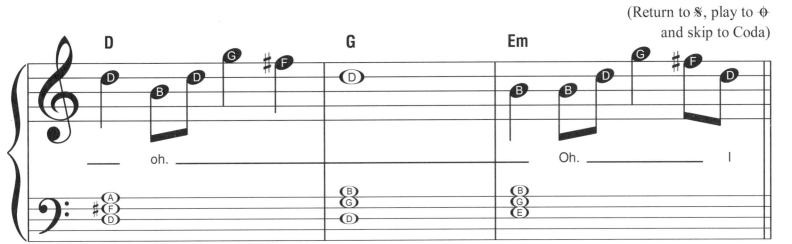

CODA

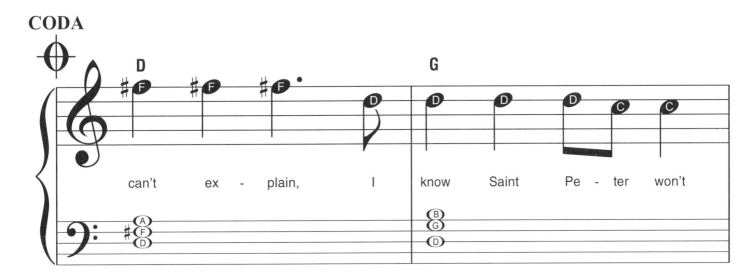

can't ex - plain, I know Saint Pe - ter won't

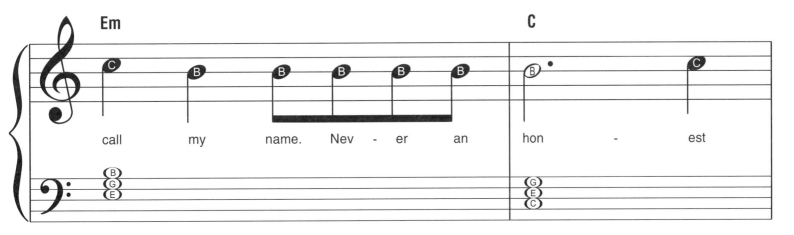

call my name. Nev - er an hon - est

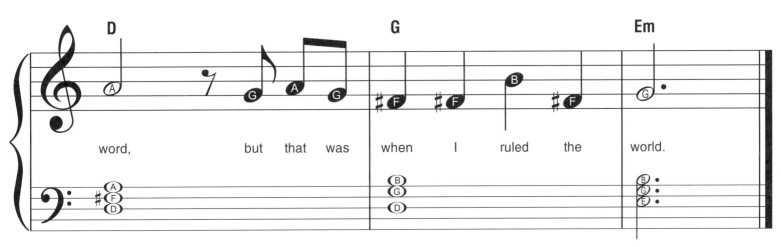

word, but that was when I ruled the world.

Stay with Me

Words and Music by Sam Smith,
James Napier, William Edward Phillips,
Tom Petty and Jeff Lynne

Moderately slow

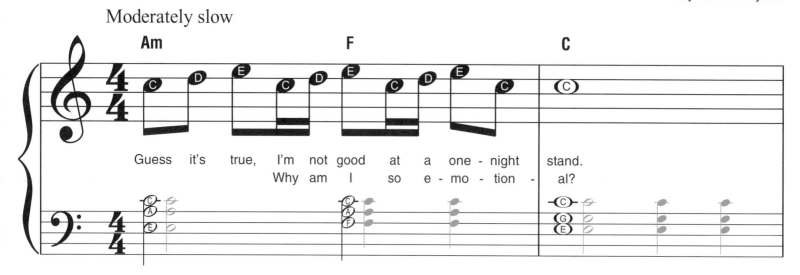

Guess it's true, I'm not good at a one-night stand.
Why am I so e - mo - tion - al?

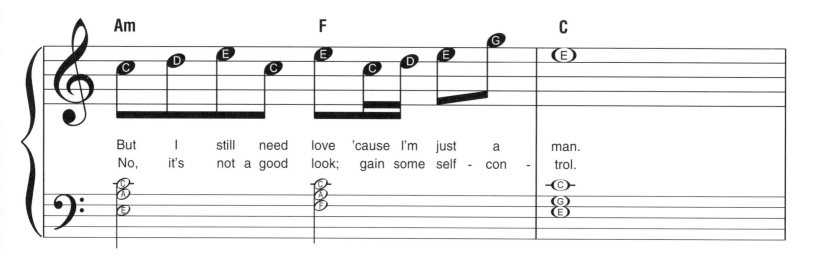

But I still need love 'cause I'm just a man.
No, it's not a good look; gain some self - con - trol.

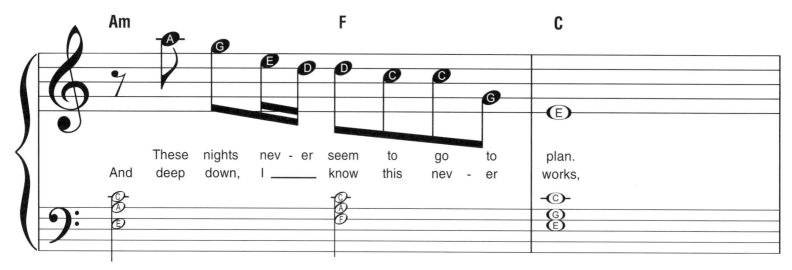

These nights nev-er seem to go to plan.
And deep down, I _____ know this nev - er works,

Thinking Out Loud

Words and Music by Ed Sheeran
and Amy Wadge

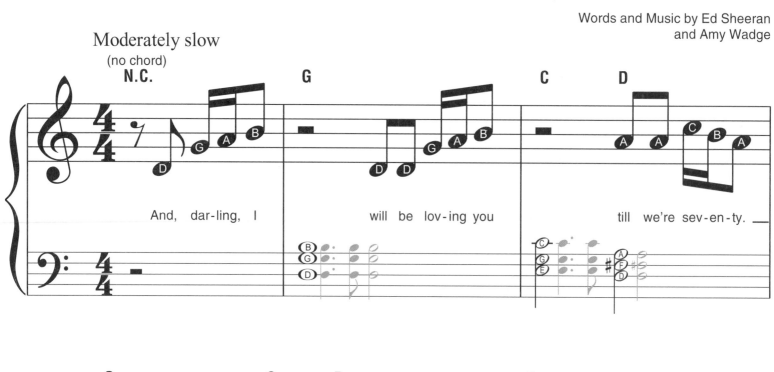

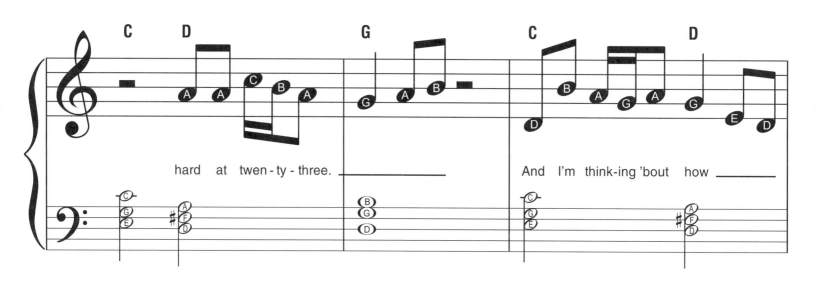

What Makes You Beautiful

Words and Music by Savan Kotecha,
Rami Yacoub and Carl Falk

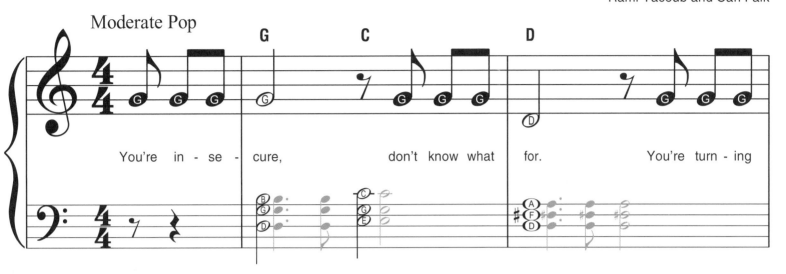

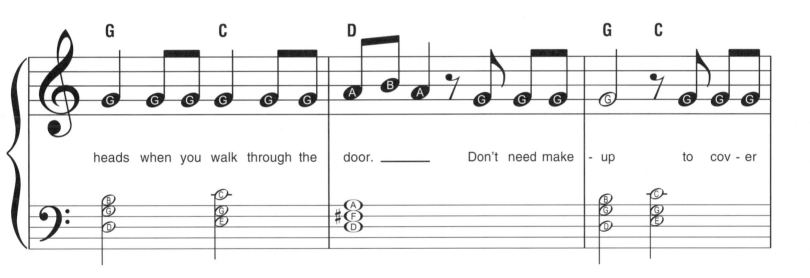

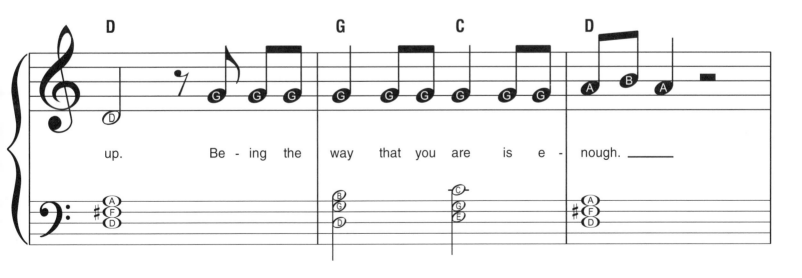

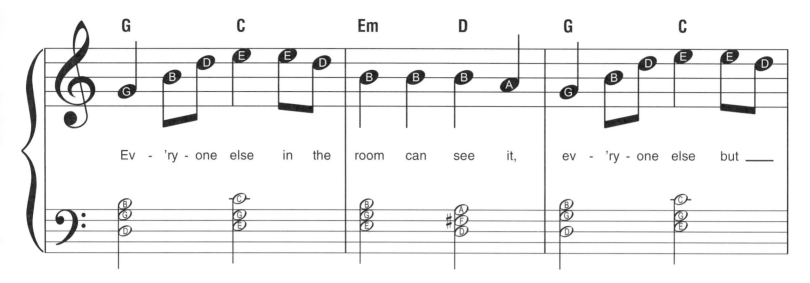

Ev - 'ry - one else in the room can see it, ev - 'ry - one else but ___

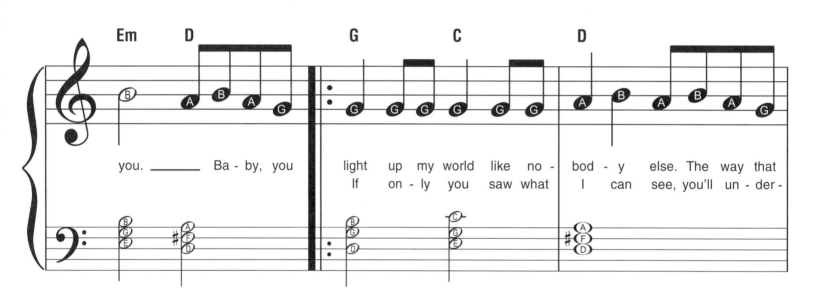

you. ___ Ba - by, you

If on - ly you saw what

light up my world like no - bod - y else. The way that

I can see, you'll un - der -

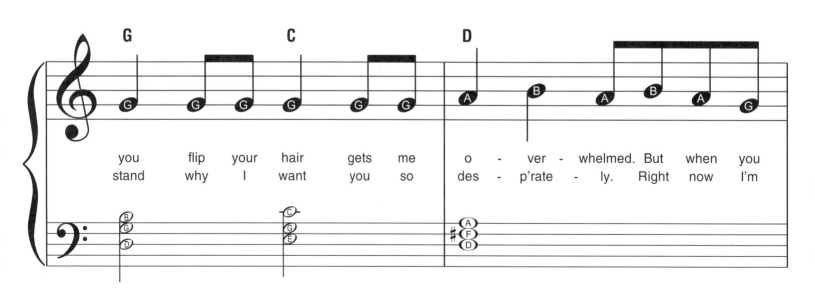

you flip your hair gets me

stand why I want you so

o - ver - whelmed. But when you

des - p'rate - ly. Right now I'm

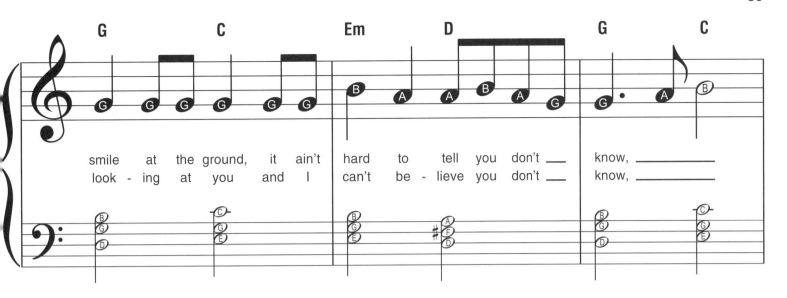

smile at the ground, it ain't hard to tell you don't ___ know, _____
look - ing at you and I can't be - lieve you don't ___ know, _____

you don't know you're beau - ti - ful.

you don't know you're beau - ti - ful.

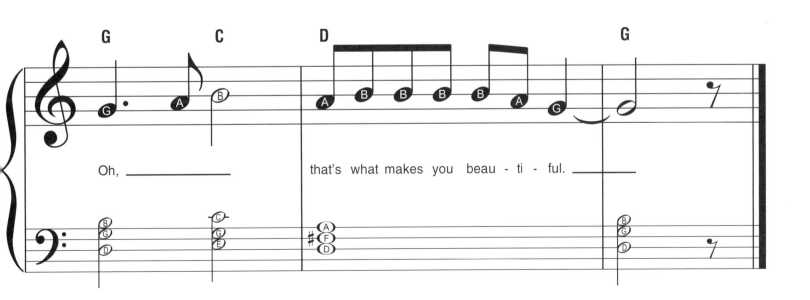

Oh, _____ that's what makes you beau - ti - ful. _____

You Are the Reason

Words and Music by Calum Scott,
Corey Sanders and Jonathan Maguire

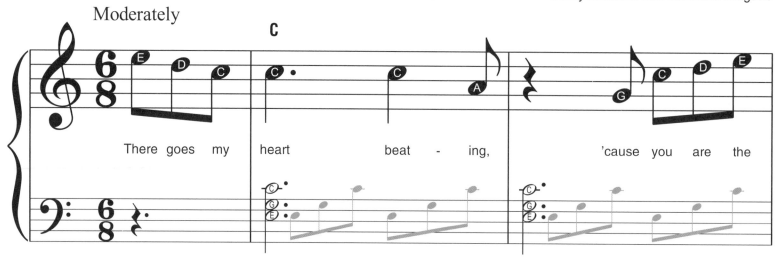

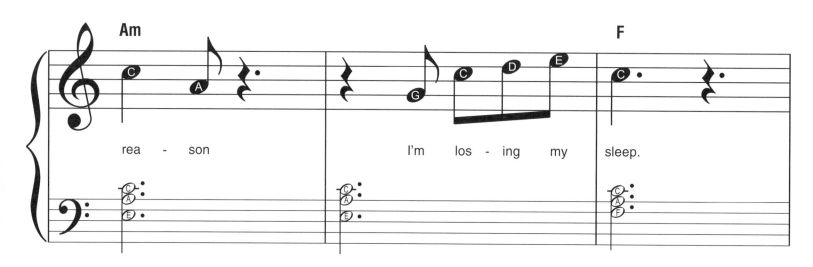

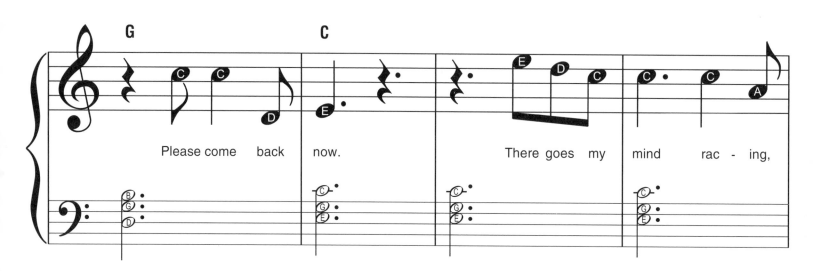

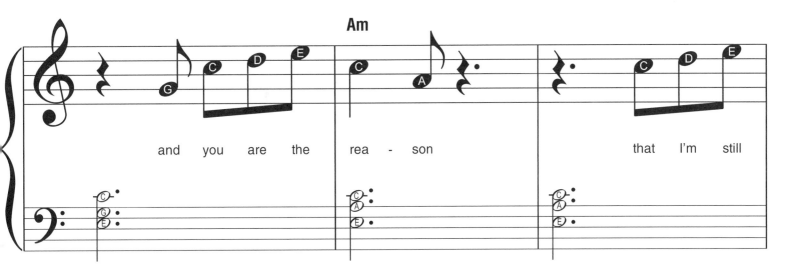

and you are the rea - son   that I'm still

breath - ing.   I'm hope - less now.   I'd climb ev - 'ry

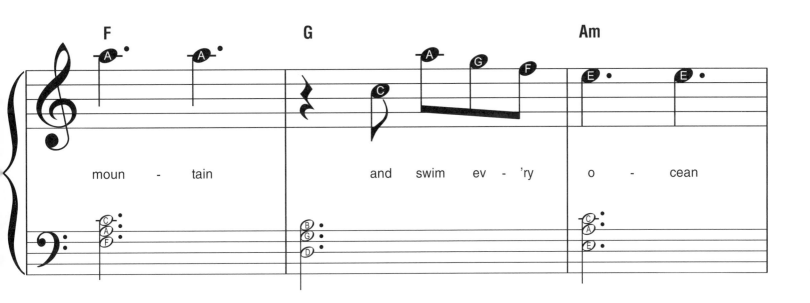

moun - tain   and swim ev - 'ry   o - cean

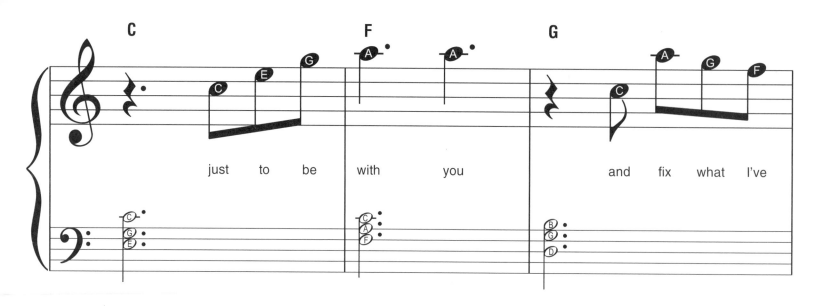

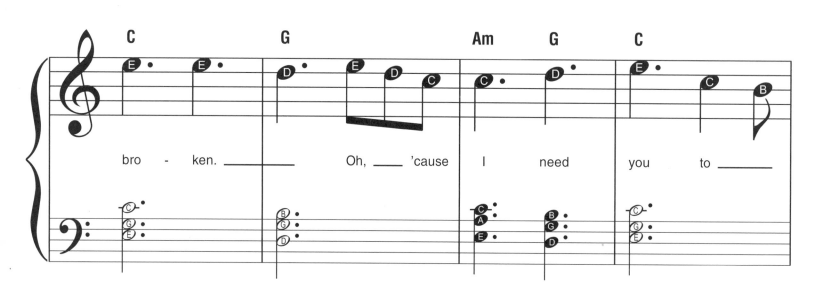

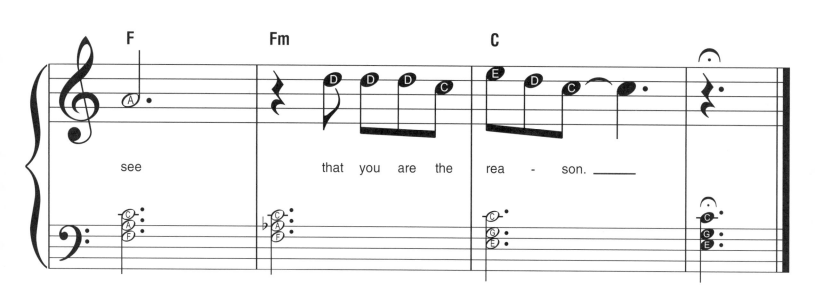

INSTANT Piano Songs

Audio Access
Included

The ***Instant Piano Songs*** series will help you play your favorite songs quickly and easily — whether you use one hand or two! Start with the melody in your right hand, adding basic left-hand chords when you're ready. Letter names inside each note speed up the learning process, and optional rhythm patterns take your playing to the next level. Online backing tracks are also included. Stream or download the tracks using the unique code inside each book, then play along to build confidence and sound great!

THE BEATLES
All My Loving · Blackbird · Can't Buy Me Love · Eleanor Rigby · Get Back · Here, There and Everywhere · Hey Jude · I Will · Let It Be · Michelle · Nowhere Man · Ob-La-Di, Ob-La-Da · Penny Lane · When I'm Sixty-Four · With a Little Help from My Friends · Yesterday · and more.
00295926 Book/Online Audio $14.99

BROADWAY'S BEST
All I Ask of You · Bring Him Home · Defying Gravity · Don't Cry for Me Argentina · Edelweiss · Memory · The Music of the Night · On My Own · People · Seasons of Love · Send in the Clowns · She Used to Be Mine · Sunrise, Sunset · Tonight · Waving Through a Window · and more.
00323342 Book/Online Audio $14.99

CHRISTMAS CLASSICS
Angels We Have Heard on High · Away in a Manger · Deck the Hall · The First Noel · Good King Wenceslas · Hark! the Herald Angels Sing · Jingle Bells · Jolly Old St. Nicholas · Joy to the World · O Christmas Tree · Up on the Housetop · We Three Kings of Orient Are · We Wish You a Merry Christmas · What Child Is This? · and more.
00348326 Book/Online Audio..................................$14.99

CHRISTMAS STANDARDS
All I Want for Christmas Is You · Christmas Time Is Here · Frosty the Snow Man · Grown-Up Christmas List · A Holly Jolly Christmas · I'll Be Home for Christmas · Jingle Bell Rock · The Little Drummer Boy · Mary, Did You Know? · Merry Christmas, Darling · Rudolph the Red-Nosed Reindeer · White Christmas · and more.
00294854 Book/Online Audio $14.99

CLASSICAL THEMES
Canon (Pachelbel) · Für Elise (Beethoven) · Jesu, Joy of Man's Desiring (Bach) · Jupiter (Holst) · Lullaby (Brahms) · Pomp and Circumstance (Elgar) · Spring (Vivaldi) · Symphony No. 9, Fourth Movement ("Ode to Joy") (Beethoven) · and more.
00283826 Book/Online Audio..................................$14.99

DISNEY FAVORITES
Beauty and the Beast · Can You Feel the Love Tonight · Chim Chim Cher-ee · Colors of the Wind · A Dream Is a Wish Your Heart Makes · Friend Like Me · How Far I'll Go · It's a Small World · Kiss the Girl · Lava · Let It Go · Mickey Mouse March · Part of Your World · Reflection · Remember Me (Ernesto de la Cruz) · A Whole New World · You'll Be in My Heart (Pop Version) · and more.
00283720 Book/Online Audio..................................$14.99

HITS OF 2010-2019
All About That Bass (Meghan Trainor) · All of Me (John Legend) · Can't Stop the Feeling (Justin Timberlake) · Happy (Pharrell Williams) · Hey, Soul Sister (Train) · Just the Way You Are (Bruno Mars) · Rolling in the Deep (Adele) · Shallow (Lady Gaga & Bradley Cooper) · Shake It Off (Taylor Swift) · Shape of You (Ed Sheeran) · and more.
00345364 Book/Online Audio..................................$14.99

KIDS' POP SONGS
Adore You (Harry Styles) · Cool Kids (AJR) · Drivers License (Olivia Rodrigo) · How Far I'll Go (from Moana) · A Million Dreams (from The Greatest Showman) · Ocean Eyes (Billie Eilish) · Shake It Off (Taylor Swift) · What Makes You Beautiful (One Direction) · and more.
00371694 Book/Online Audio..................................$14.99

MOVIE SONGS
As Time Goes By · City of Stars · Endless Love · Hallelujah · I Will Always Love You · Laura · Moon River · My Heart Will Go on (Love Theme from 'Titanic') · Over the Rainbow · Singin' in the Rain · Skyfall · Somewhere Out There · Stayin' Alive · Tears in Heaven · Unchained Melody · Up Where We Belong · The Way We Were · What a Wonderful World · and more.
00283718 Book/Online Audio..................................$14.99

POP HITS
All of Me · Chasing Cars · Despacito · Feel It Still · Havana · Hey, Soul Sister · Ho Hey · I'm Yours · Just Give Me a Reason · Love Yourself · Million Reasons · Perfect · Riptide · Shake It Off · Stay with Me · Thinking Out Loud · Viva La Vida · What Makes You Beautiful · and more.
00283825 Book/Online Audio..................................$15.99

SONGS FOR KIDS
Do-Re-Mi · Hakuna Matata · It's a Small World · On Top of Spaghetti · Puff the Magic Dragon · The Rainbow Connection · SpongeBob SquarePants Theme Song · Take Me Out to the Ball Game · Tomorrow · The Wheels on the Bus · Won't You Be My Neighbor? (It's a Beautiful Day in the Neighborhood) · You Are My Sunshine · and more.
00323352 Book/Online Audio..................................$15.99

www.halleonard.com

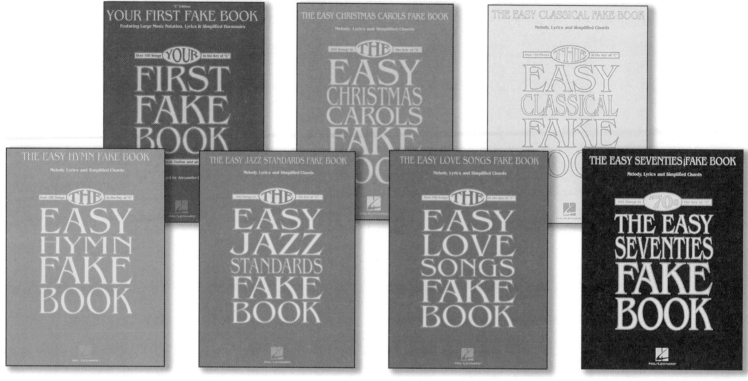

Big Fun with Big-Note Piano Books!

These songbooks feature exciting easy arrangements for beginning piano students.

Beatles' Best
27 classics for beginners to enjoy, including: Can't Buy Me Love • Eleanor Rigby • Hey Jude • Michelle • Here, There and Everywhere • When I'm Sixty-Four • Yesterday • and more.
00222561..$17.99

The Best Songs Ever
70 favorites, featuring: Body and Soul • Crazy • Edelweiss • Fly Me to the Moon • Georgia on My Mind • Imagine • The Lady Is a Tramp • Memory • A String of Pearls • Tears in Heaven • Unforgettable • You Are So Beautiful • and more.
00310425..$24.99

Chart Hits of 2020-2021
16 of the top hits of 2020 into 2021, including: Drivers License (Olivia Rodrigo) • Dynamite (BTS) • Kings & Queens (Ava Max) • Positions (Ariana Grande) • Therefore I Am (Billie Eilish) • Watermelon Sugar (Harry Styles) • Willow (Taylor Swift) • and more.
00364362..$16.99

Children's Favorite Movie Songs
arranged by Phillip Keveren
16 favorites from films, including: The Bare Necessities • Beauty and the Beast • Can You Feel the Love Tonight • Do-Re-Mi • The Rainbow Connection • Tomorrow • Zip-A-Dee-Doo-Dah • and more.
00310838..$14.99

Disney Big-Note Collection
Over 40 Disney favorites, including: Circle of Life • Colors of the Wind • Hakuna Matata • It's a Small World • Under the Sea • A Whole New World • Winnie the Pooh • Zip-A-Dee-Doo-Dah • and more.
00316056..$22.99

Favorite Children's Songs
arranged by Bill Boyd
29 easy arrangements of songs to play and sing with children: Peter Cottontail • I Whistle a Happy Tune • It's a Small World • On the Good Ship Lollipop • The Rainbow Connection • and more!
00240251..$14.99

Favorite TV Themes
22 themes from the small screen, including: Addams Family Theme • Happy Days • Jeopardy Theme • Mission: Impossible Theme • Price Is Right (Opening Theme) • Sesame Street Theme • Won't You Be My Neighbor? • and more.
00294318..$10.99

Frozen
9 songs from this hit Disney film, plus full-color illustrations from the movie. Songs include the standout single "Let It Go", plus: Do You Want to Build a Snowman? • For the First Time in Forever • Reindeer(s) Are Better Than People • and more.
00126105..$15.99

The Great Big Book of Children's Songs – 2nd Edition
66 super tunes that kids adore, includes: Circle of Life • Edelweiss • If I Only Had a Brain • Over the Rainbow • Puff the Magic Dragon • Rubber Duckie • Sing • This Land Is Your Land • Under the Sea • and dozens more!
00119364..$17.99

Happy Birthday to You and Other Great Songs for Big-Note Piano
16 essential favorites, including: Chitty Chitty Bang Bang • Good Night • Happy Birthday to You • Heart and Soul • Over the Rainbow • Sing • This Land Is Your Land • and more.
00119636..$9.99

Modern Movie Favorites
Beginning pianists will love to play the 18 familiar movie hits in this collection, including: The Bare Necessities • Can't Stop the Feeling • City of Stars • How Far I'll Go • In Summer • Rey's Theme • Something Wild • and more.
00241880..$14.99

Pride & Prejudice
Music from the Motion Picture Soundtrack
12 piano pieces from the 2006 Oscar-nominated film: Another Dance • Darcy's Letter • Georgiana • Leaving Netherfield • Liz on Top of the World • Meryton Townhall • The Secret Life of Daydreams • Stars and Butterflies • and more.
00316125..$16.99

Songs of Peace, Hope and Love
30 inspirational and motivational songs, including: Bridge over Troubled Water • The Climb • Hallelujah • Over the Rainbow • Put a Little Love in Your Heart • What a Wonderful World • You Raise Me Up • and more.
00119634..$12.99

Star Wars
13 Selections from a Galaxy Far, Far Away
A baker's dozen of Star Wars selections by John Williams arranged by Phillip Keveren, include: Across the Stars (Love Theme from Star Wars) • The Imperial March (Darth Vader's Theme) • Luke and Leia • Rey's Theme • Star Wars (Main Theme) • and more.
00277371..$17.99

Today's Pop Hits – 3rd Edition
A great collection of current pop hits that even developing piano players will be able to enjoy. 15 songs with lyrics, including: All of Me • Happy • Hello • Pompeii • Radioactive • Roar • Shake It Off • Stay with Me • Story of My Life • and more.
00160577..$16.99

Top Hits of 2019
17 of the year's best are included in this collection for easy to read big note piano with lyrics: Gloria • I Don't Care • Lo/Hi • ME! • Old Town Road (Remix) • Senorita • Someone You Loved • Sucker • and more.
00302427..$14.99

The Big-Note Worship Book – 2nd Edition
20 selections for budding pianists looking to play their favorite worship songs: Everlasting God • Holy Is the Lord • In Christ Alone • Revelation Song • 10,000 Reasons (Bless the Lord) • Your Grace Is Enough • and more.
00267812..$14.99